# ABC Adventures Tracing Fun for Little Learners

## This Book Belongs To:

**Copyright ©2024 All rights reserved.**

**No part of this book may be reproduced, stored in a retrieval system, or transmitted, in any form, or by any means, electronic, mechanical photocopying, recording or otherwise without the prior written permission of the publishing or a license permitting restricted copying.**

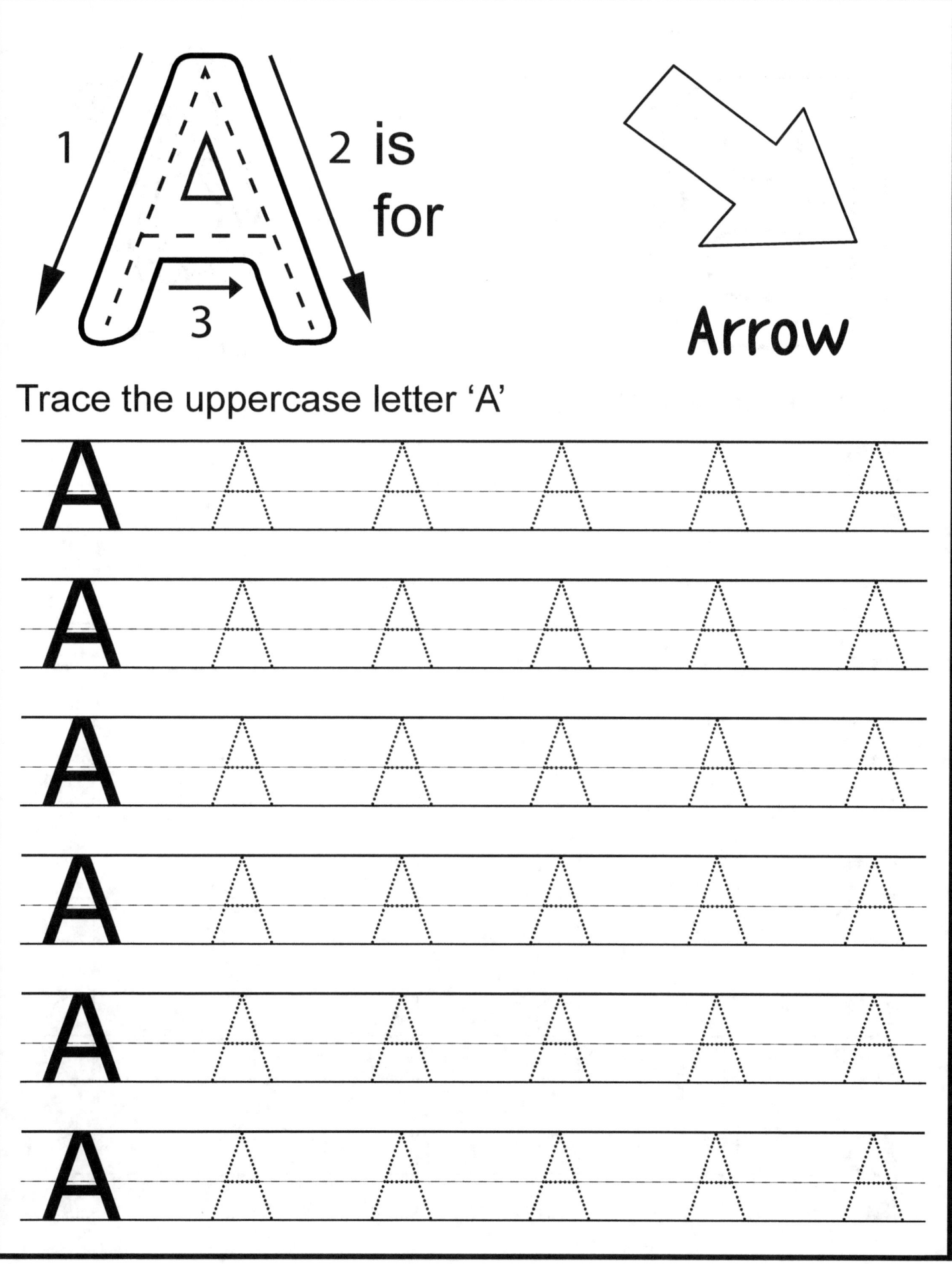

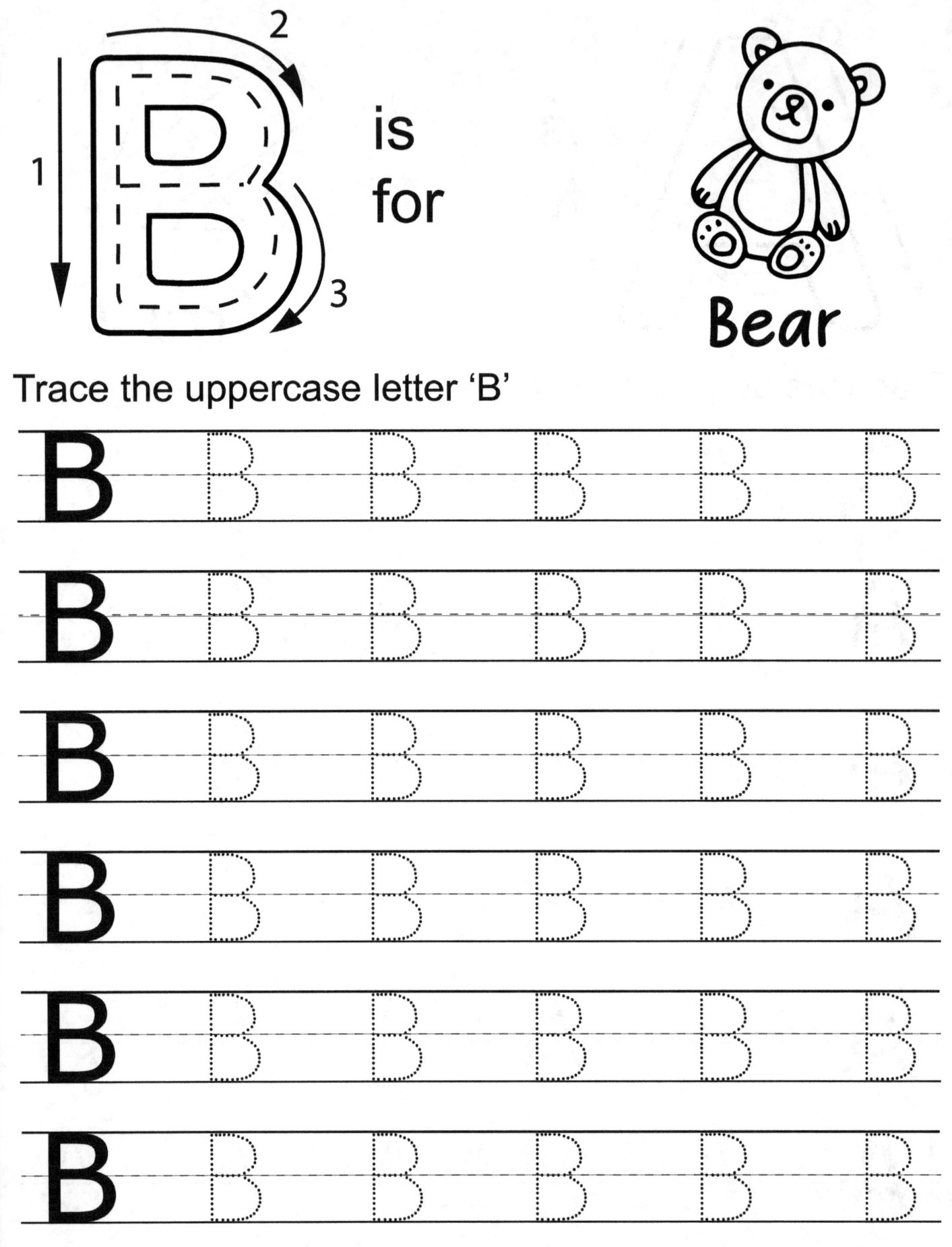

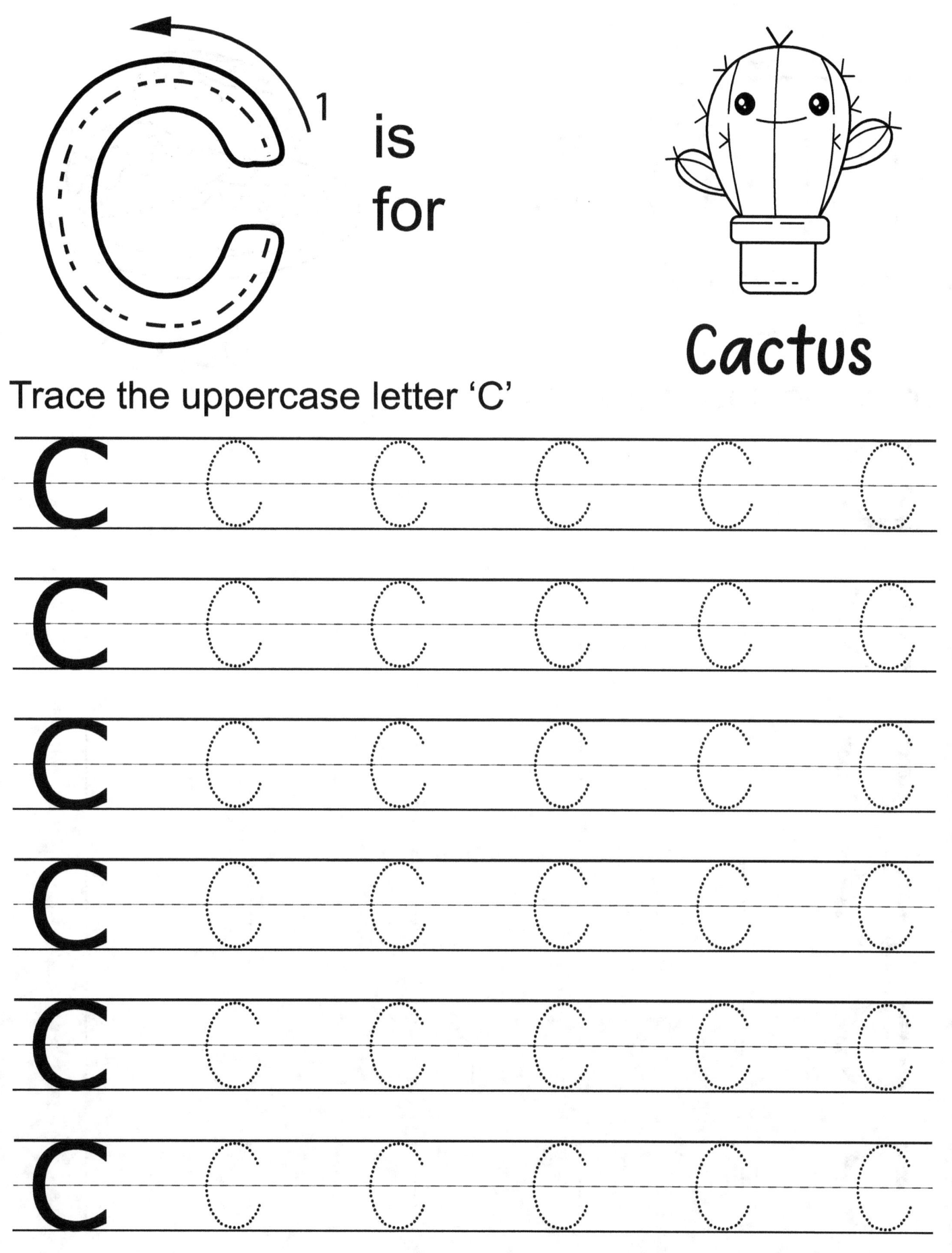

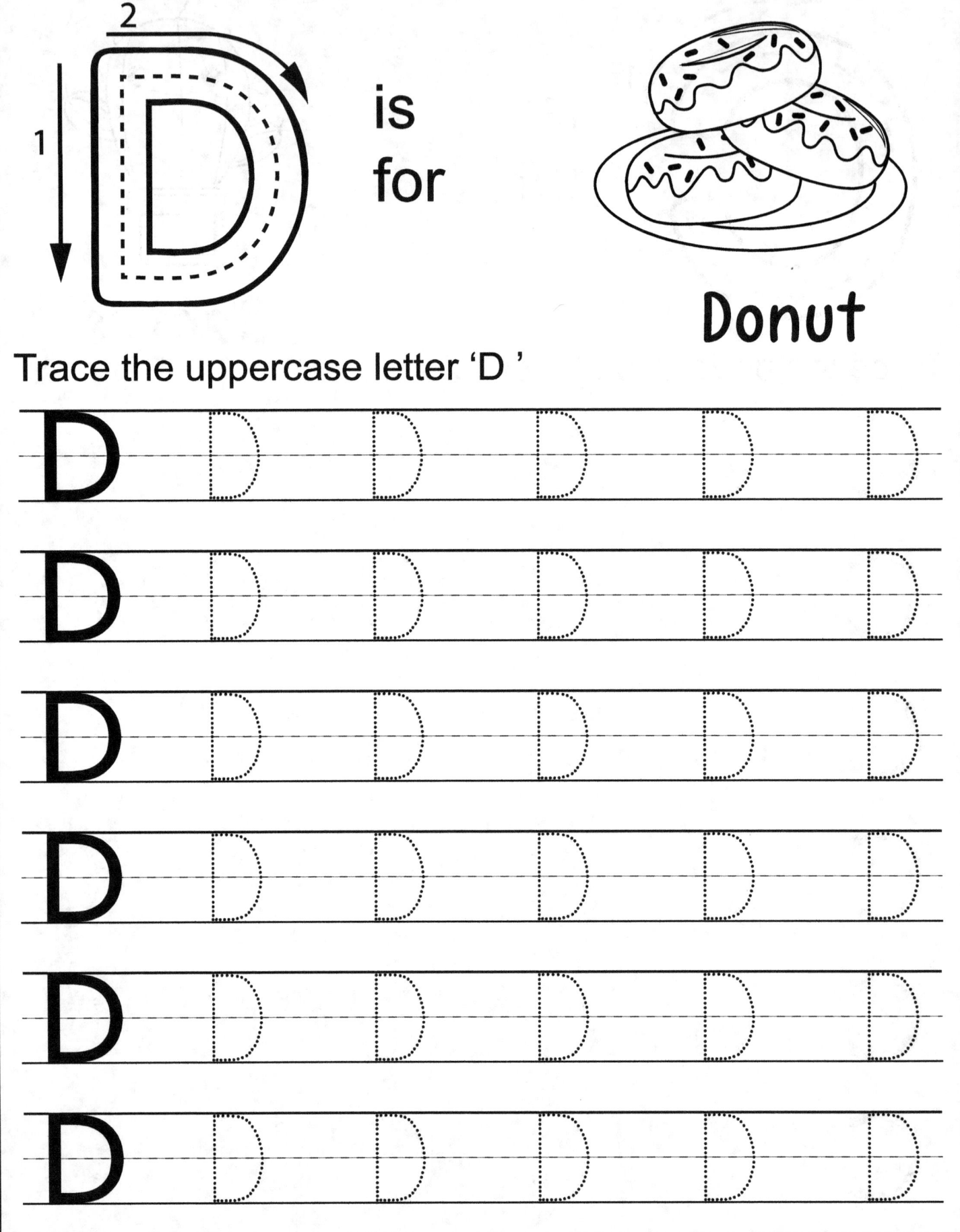

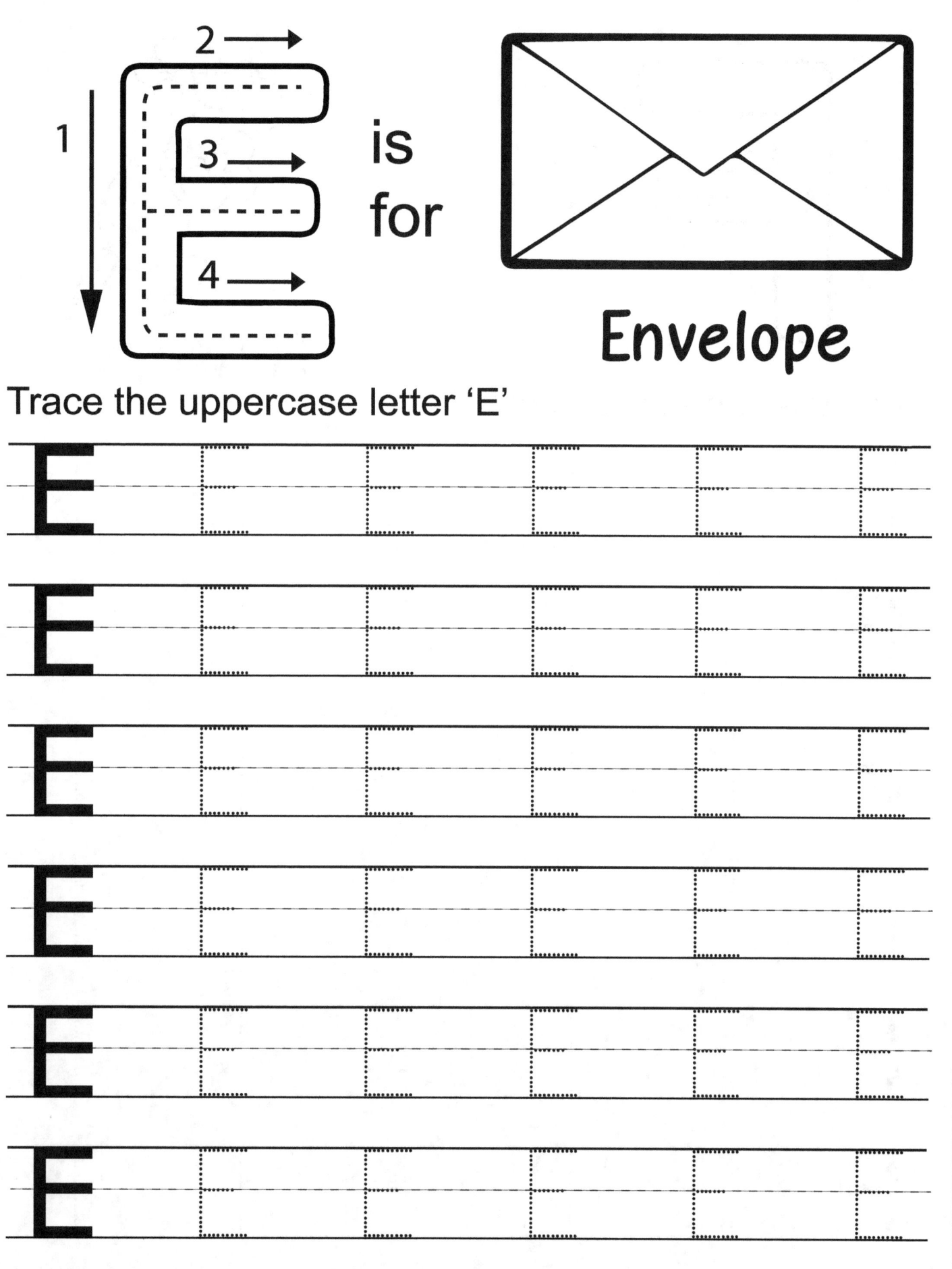

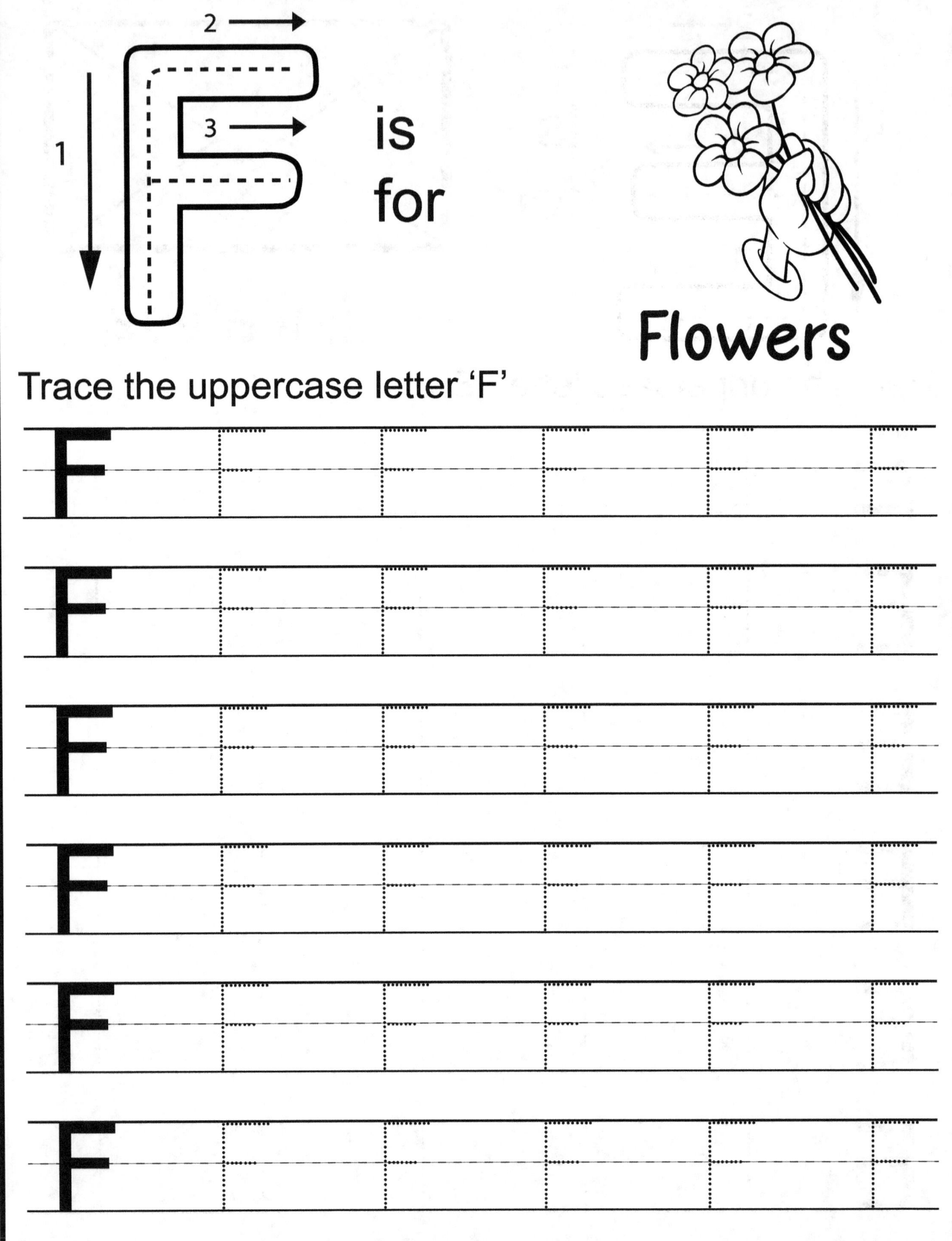

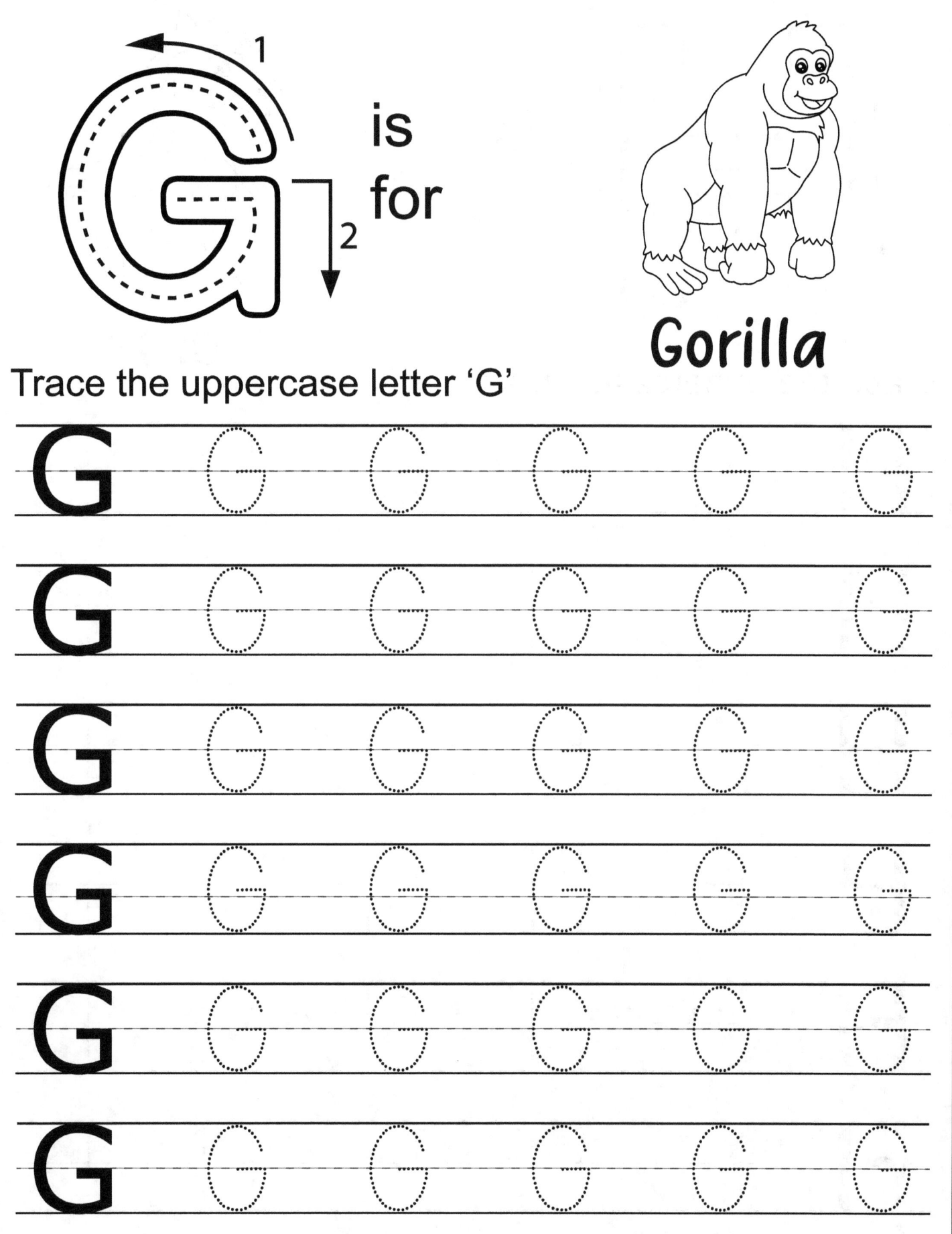

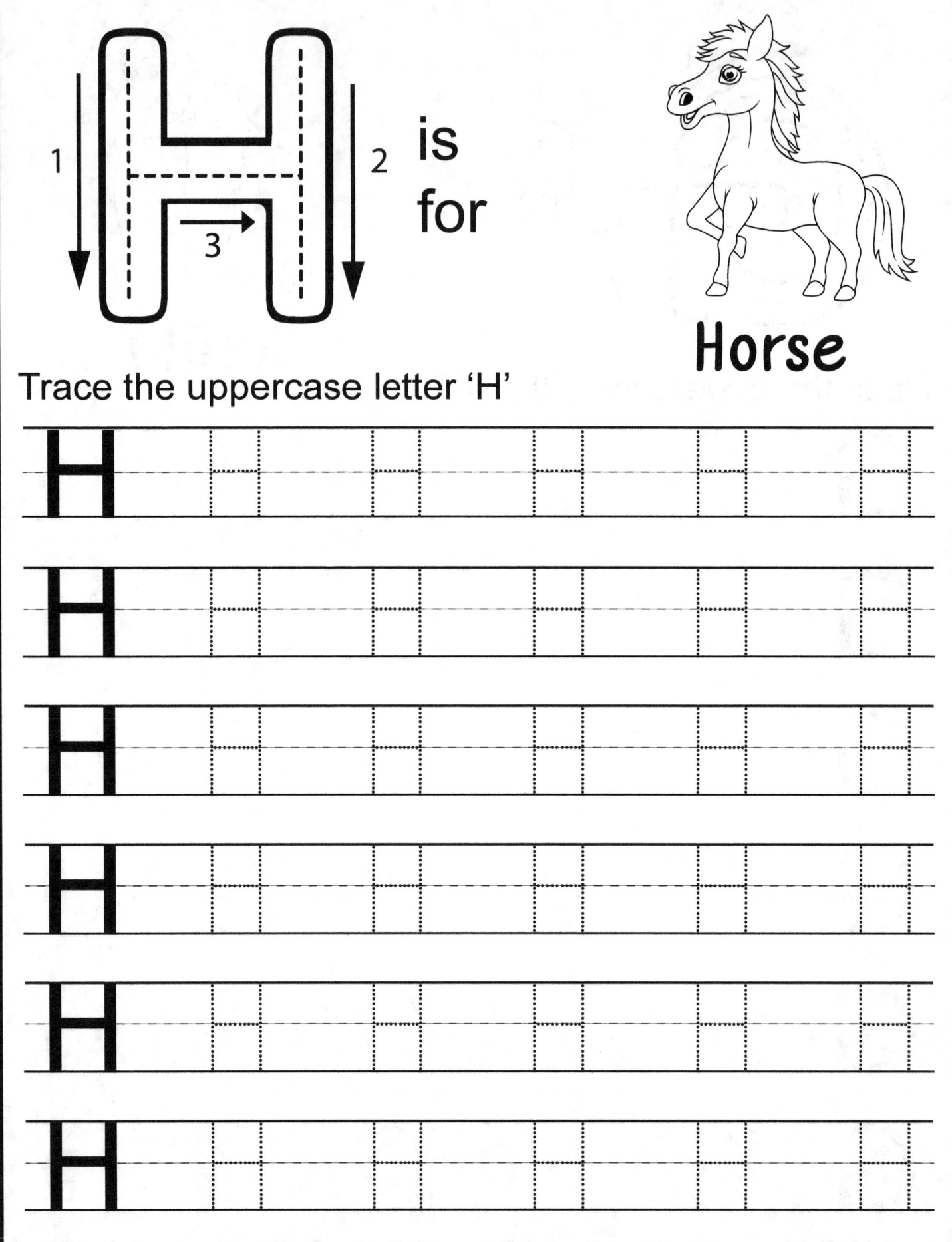

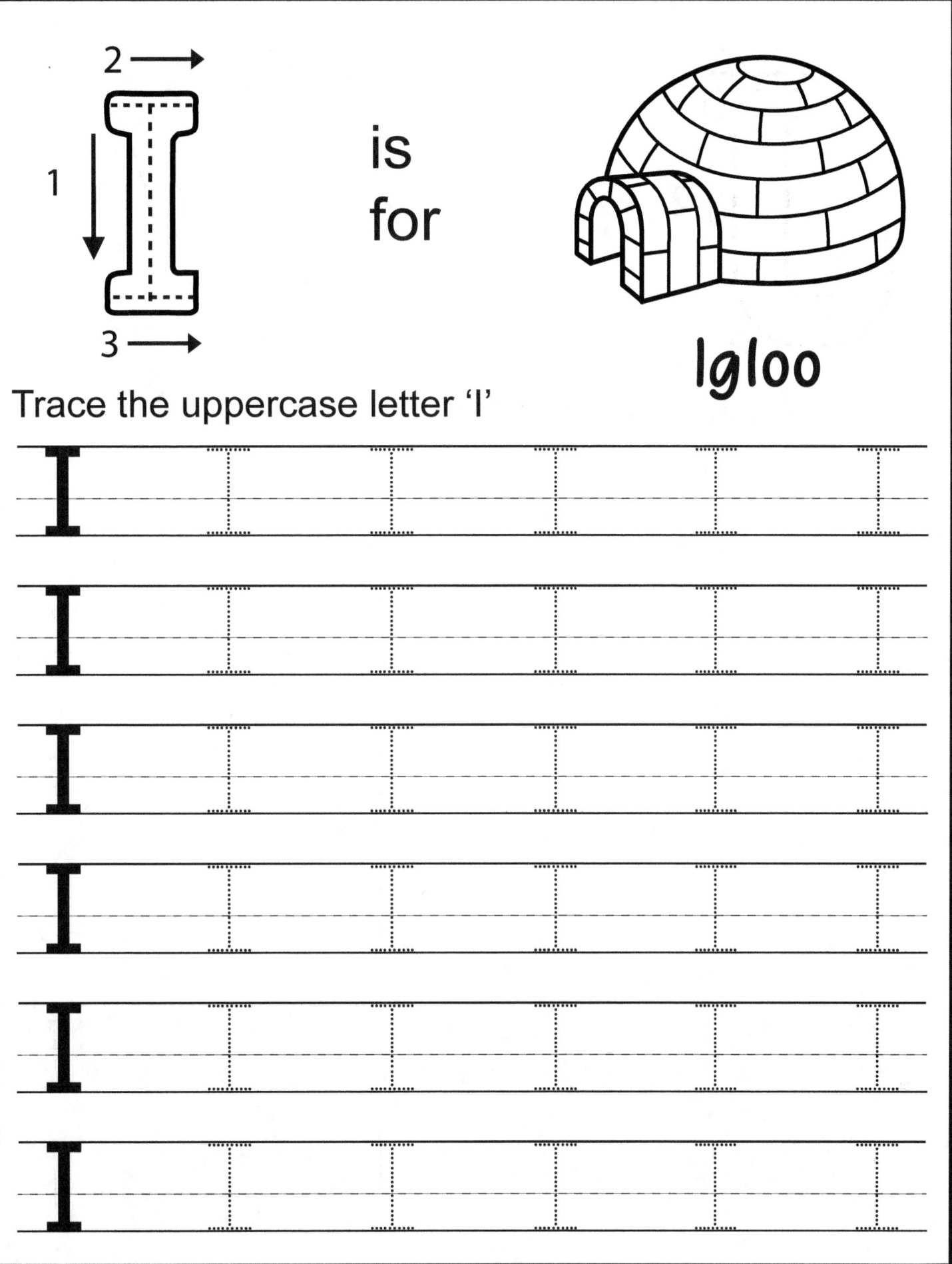

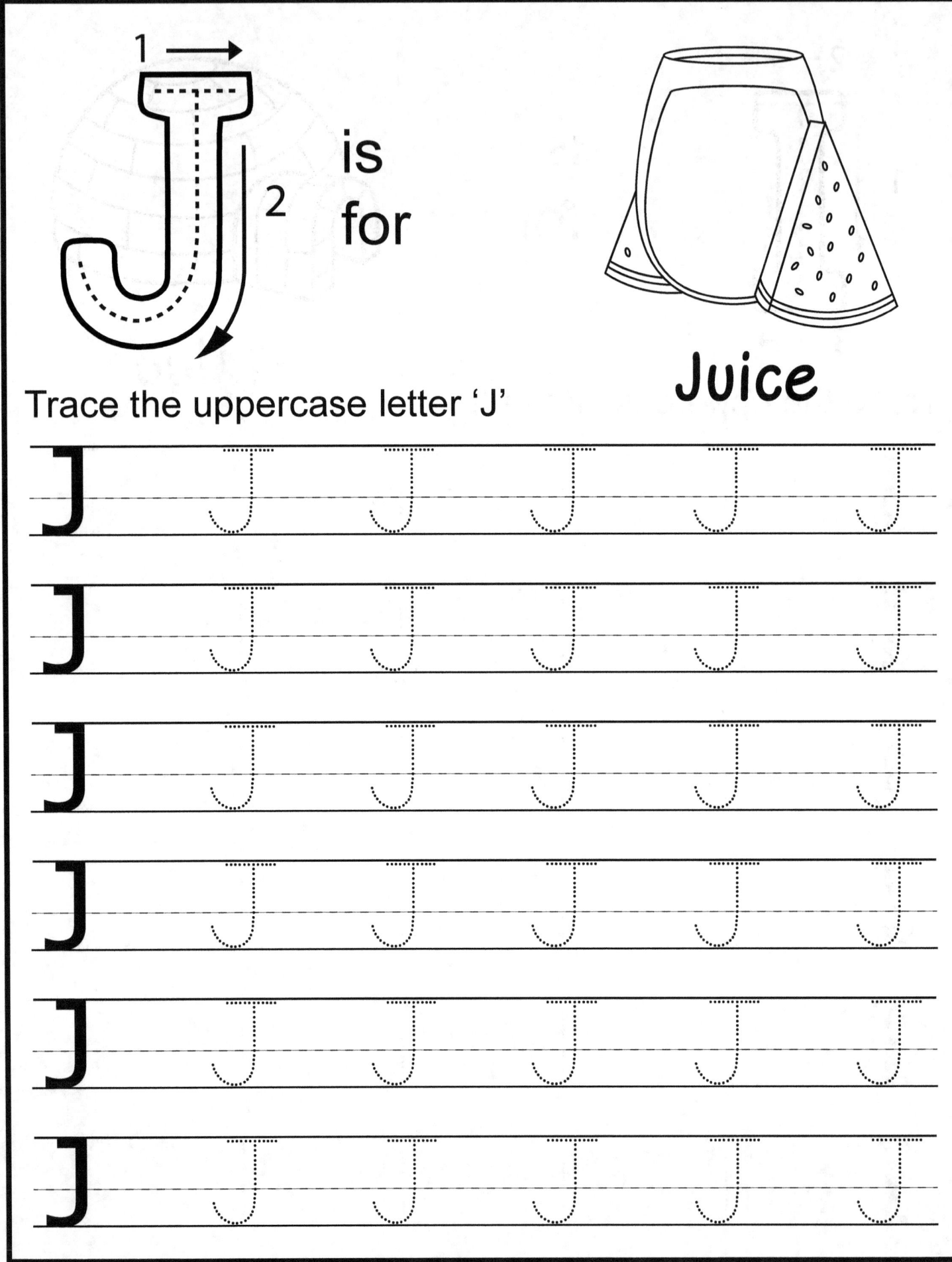

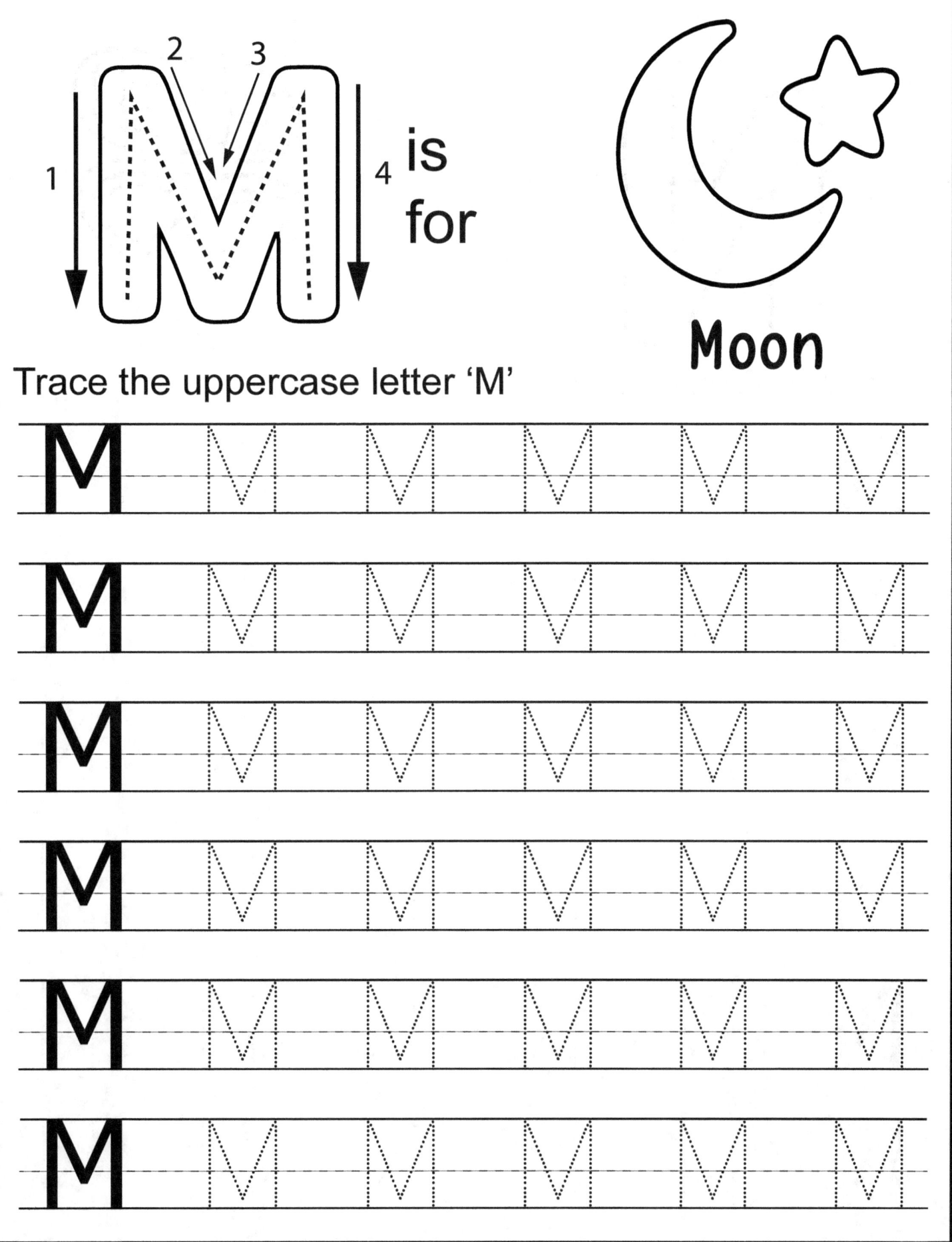

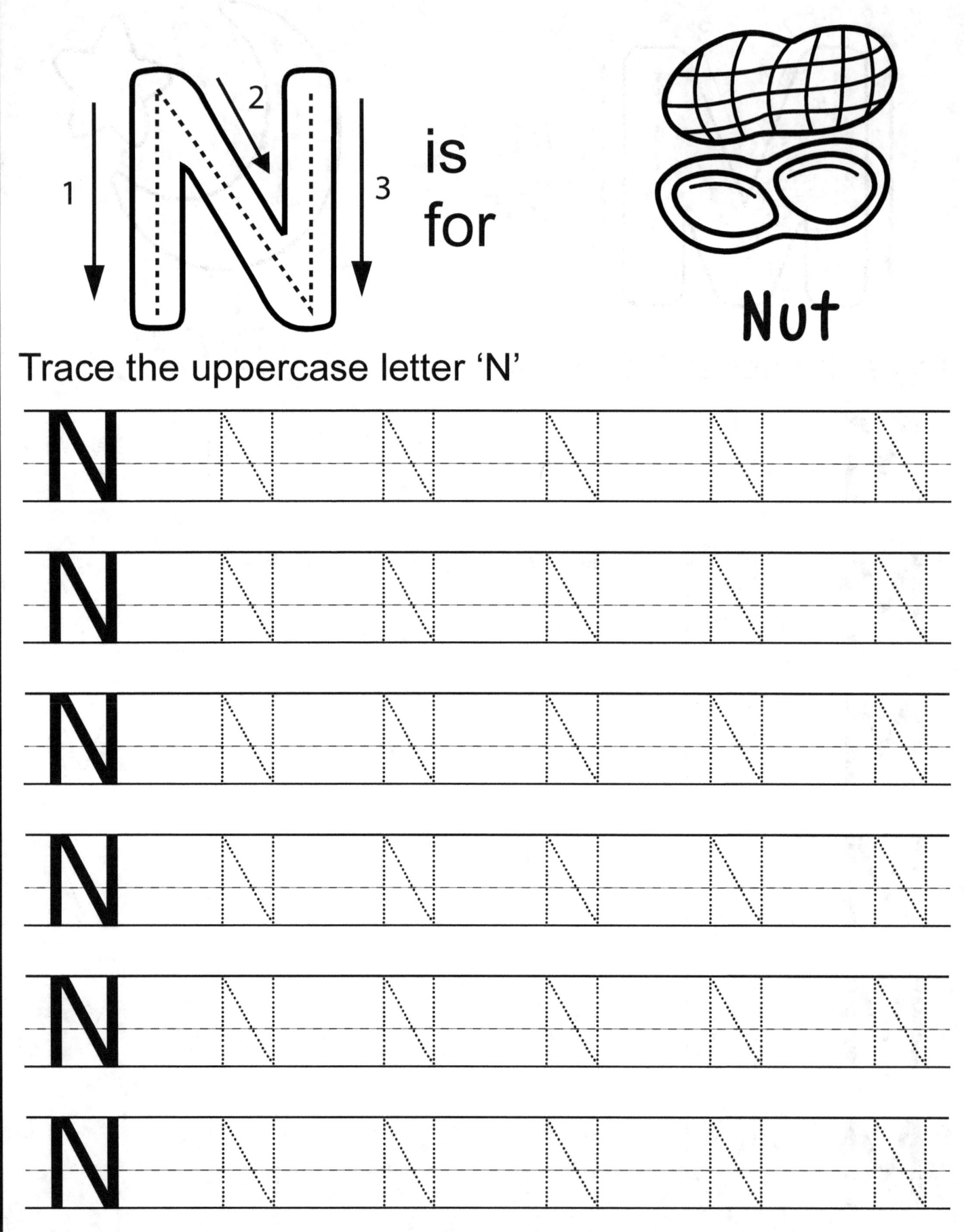

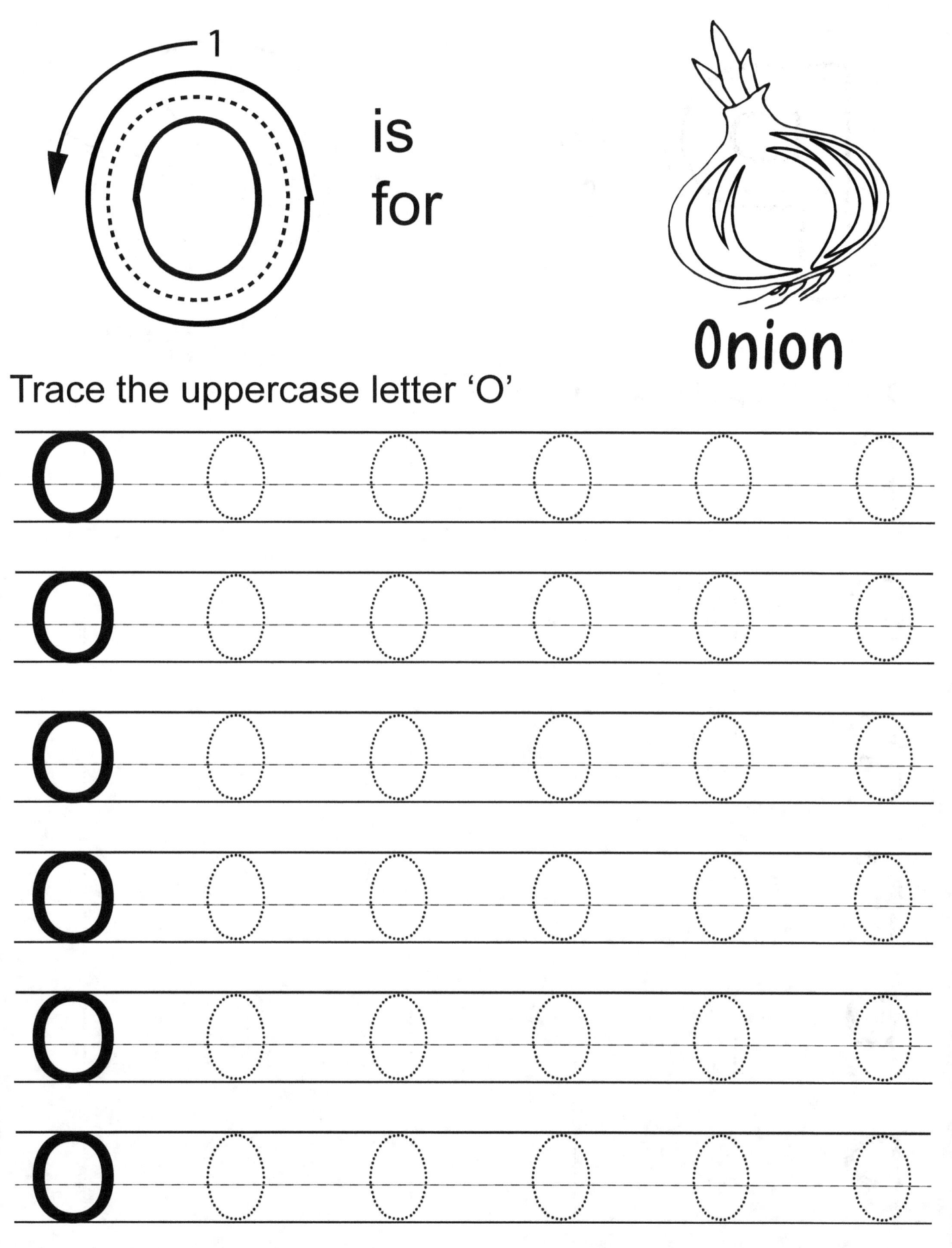

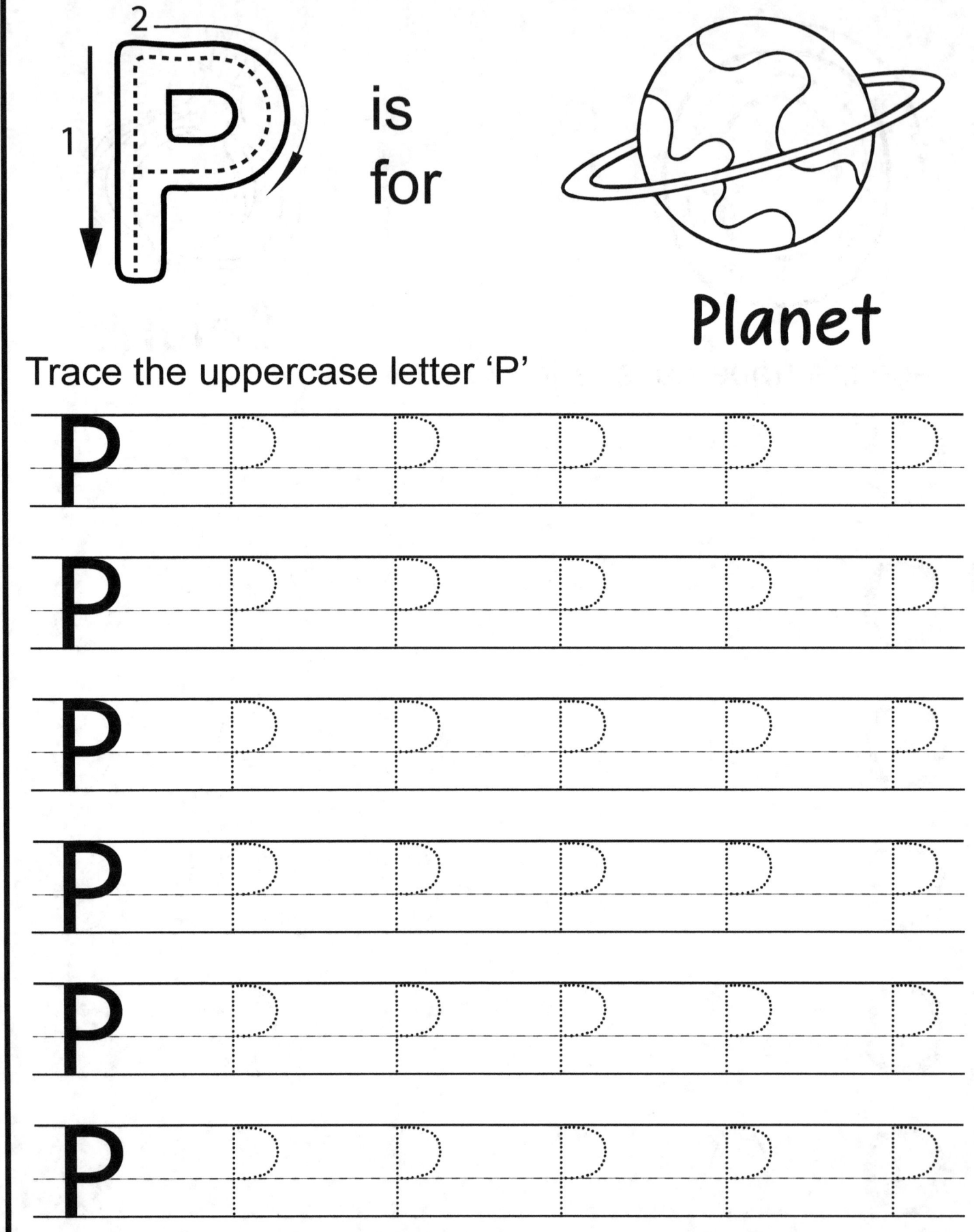

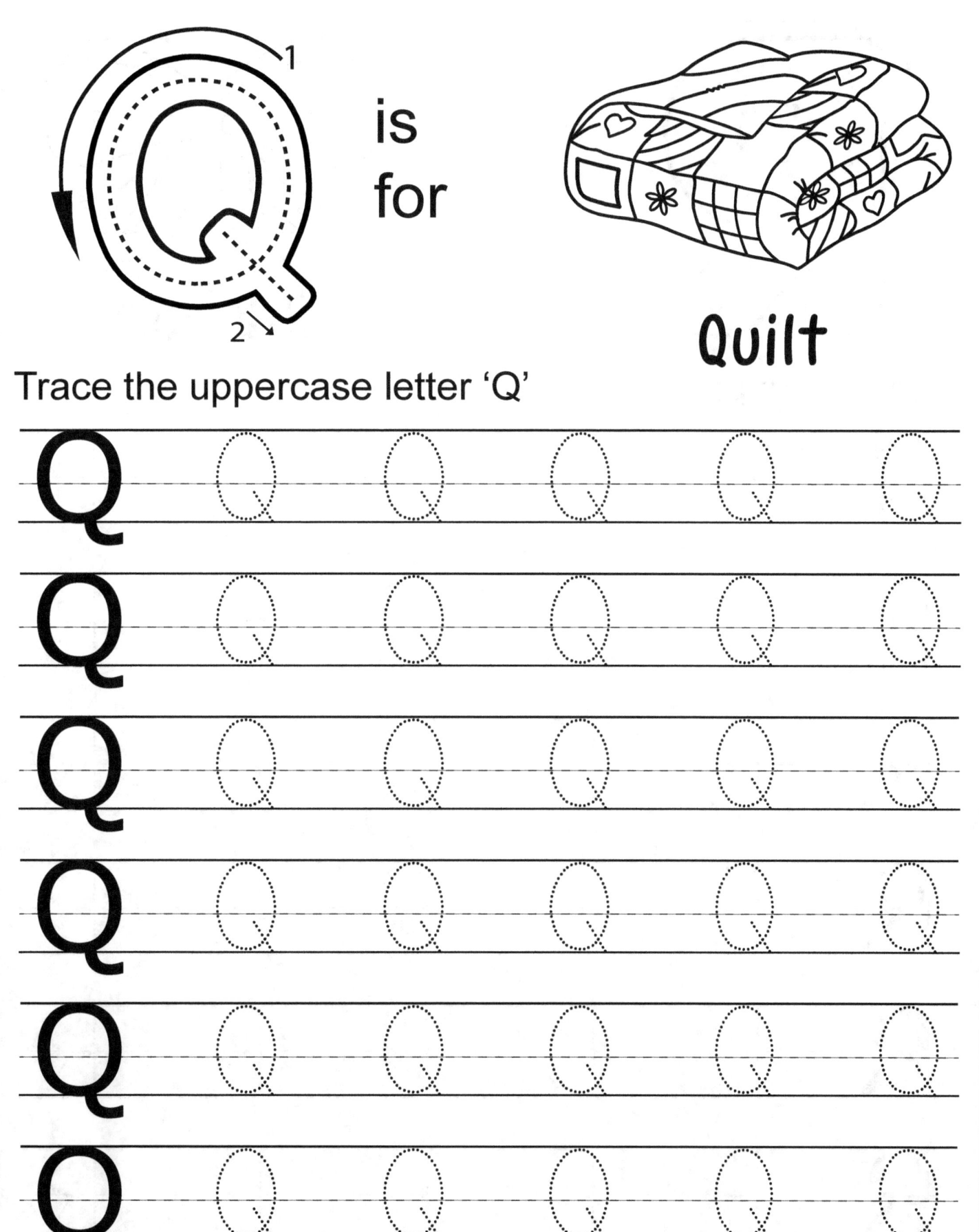

R is for Ribbon

Trace the uppercase letter 'R'

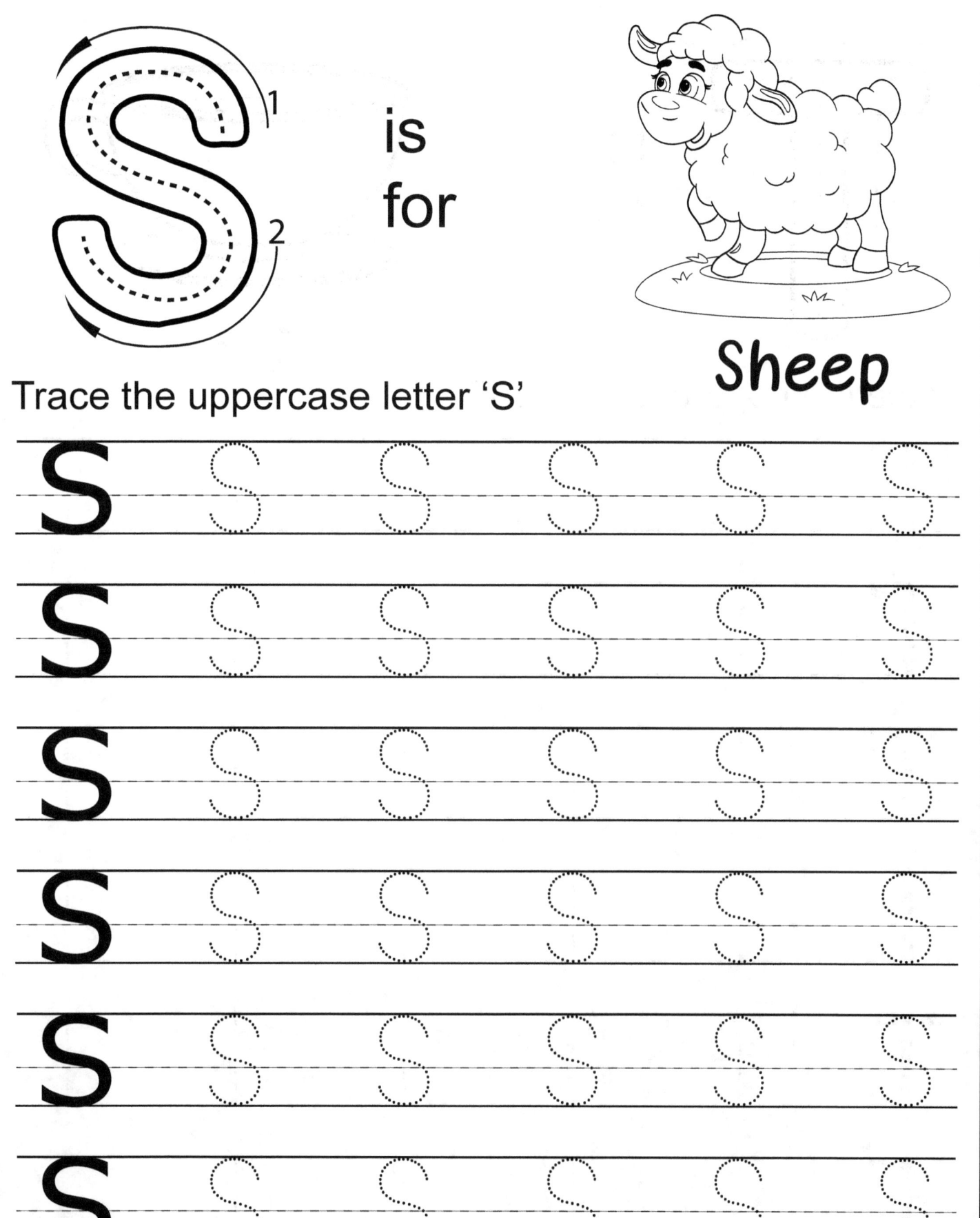

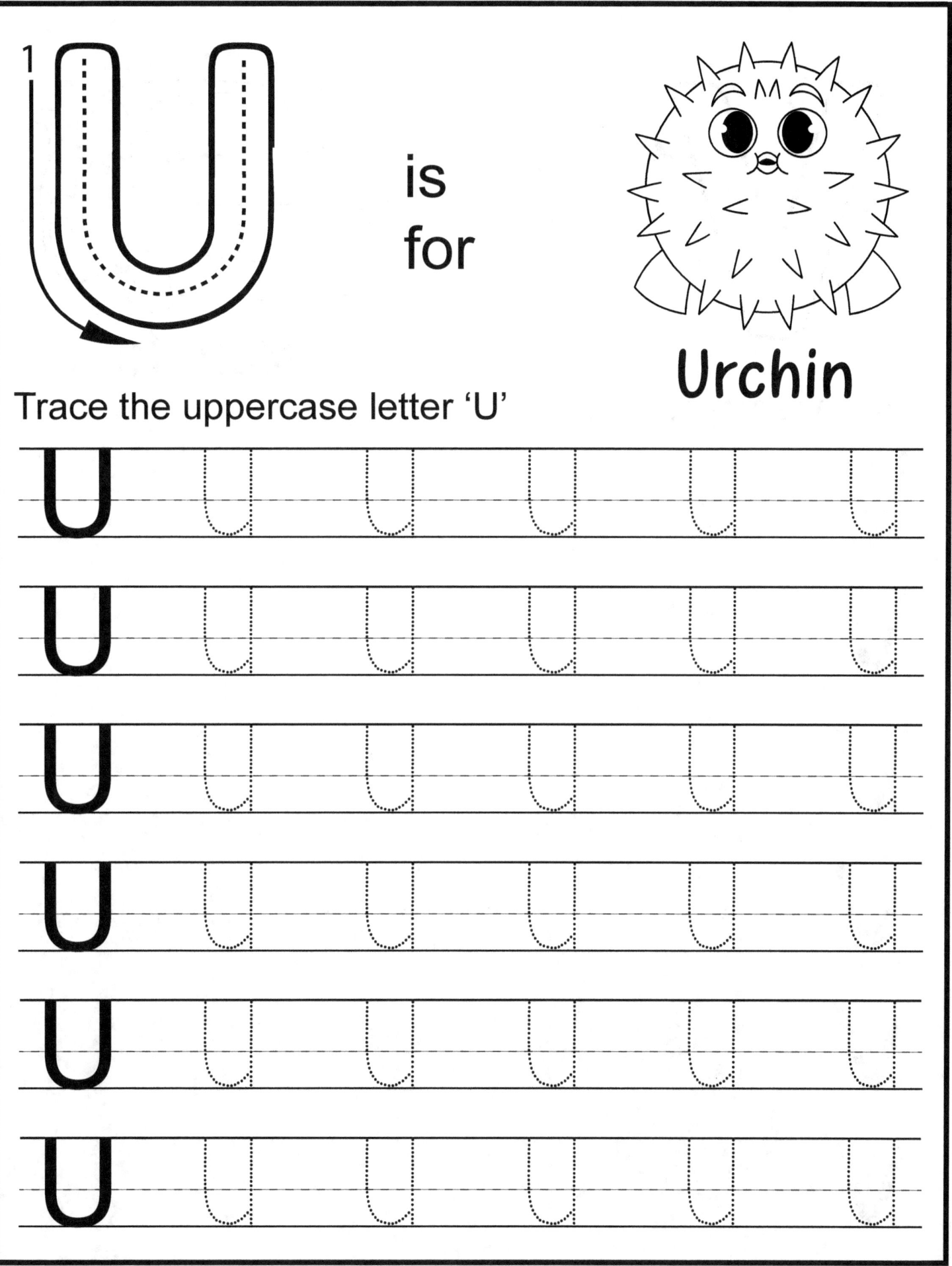

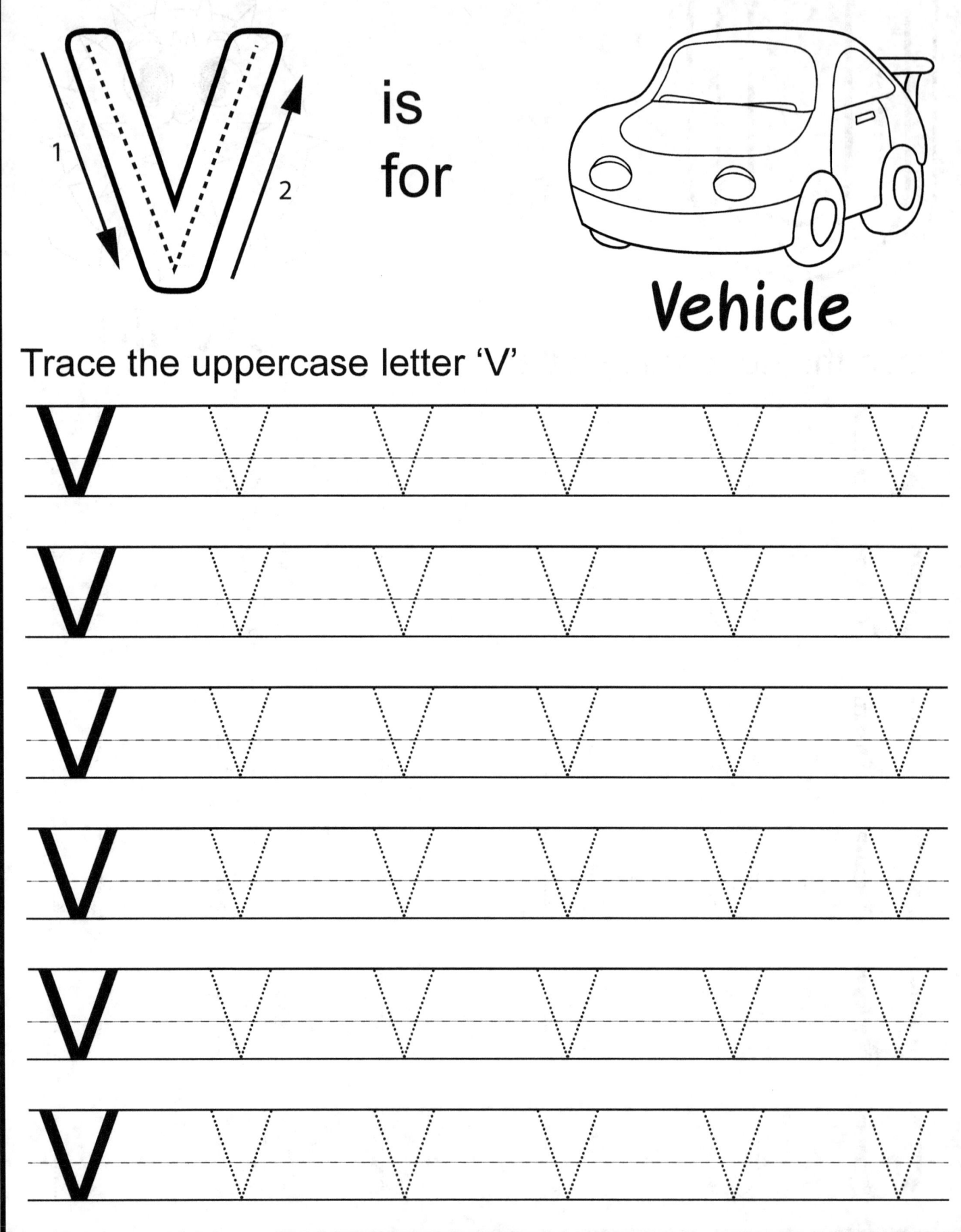

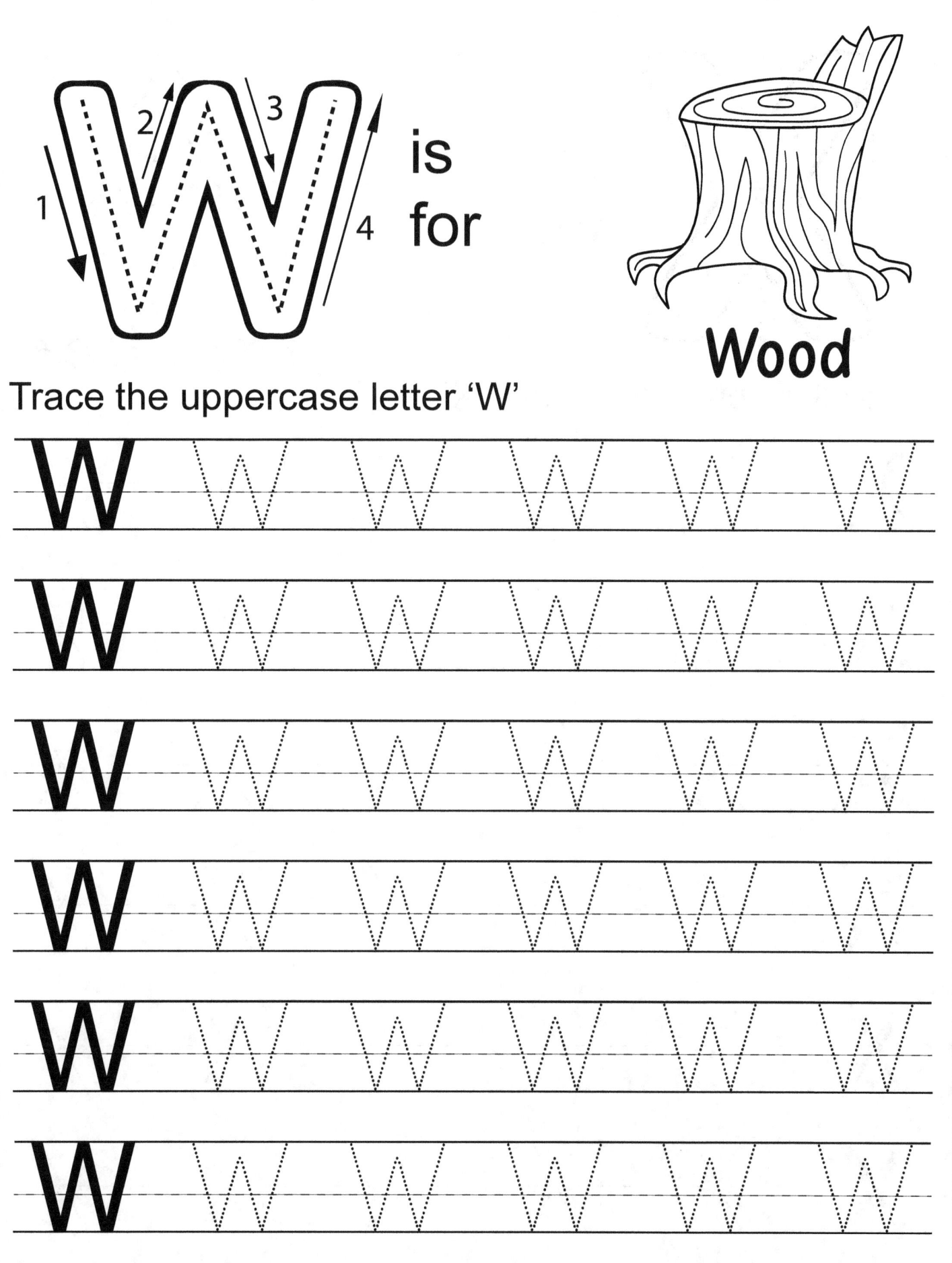

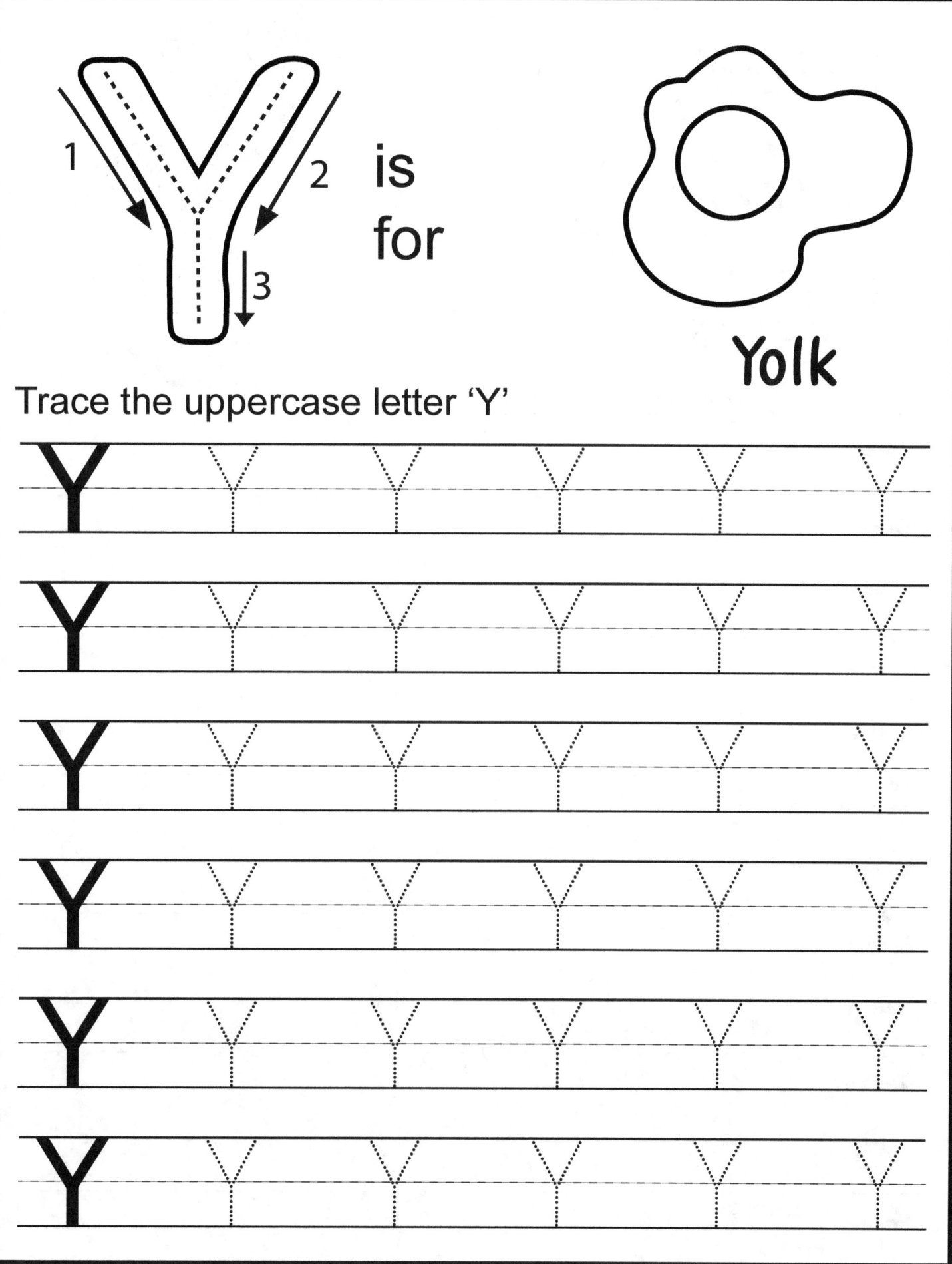

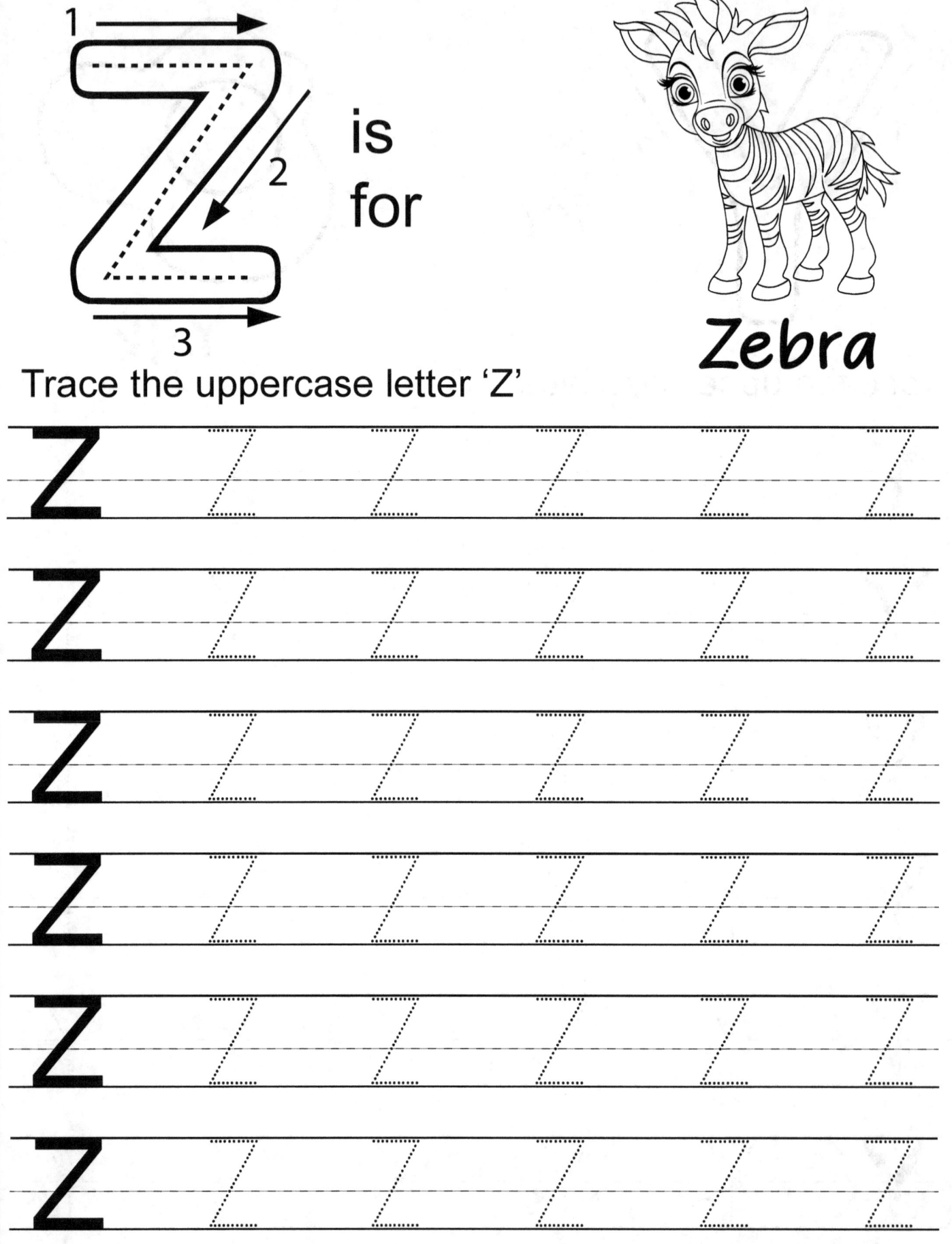

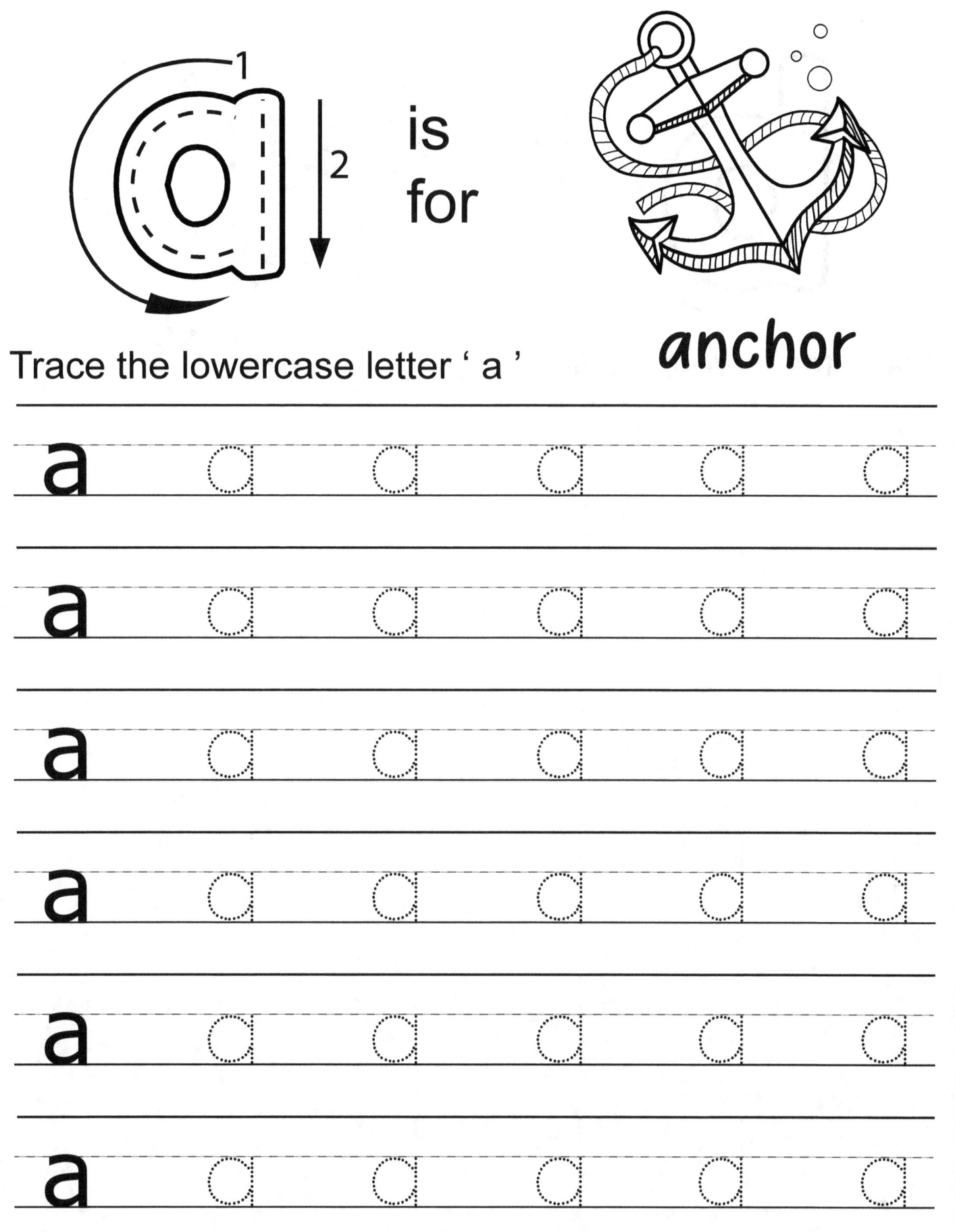

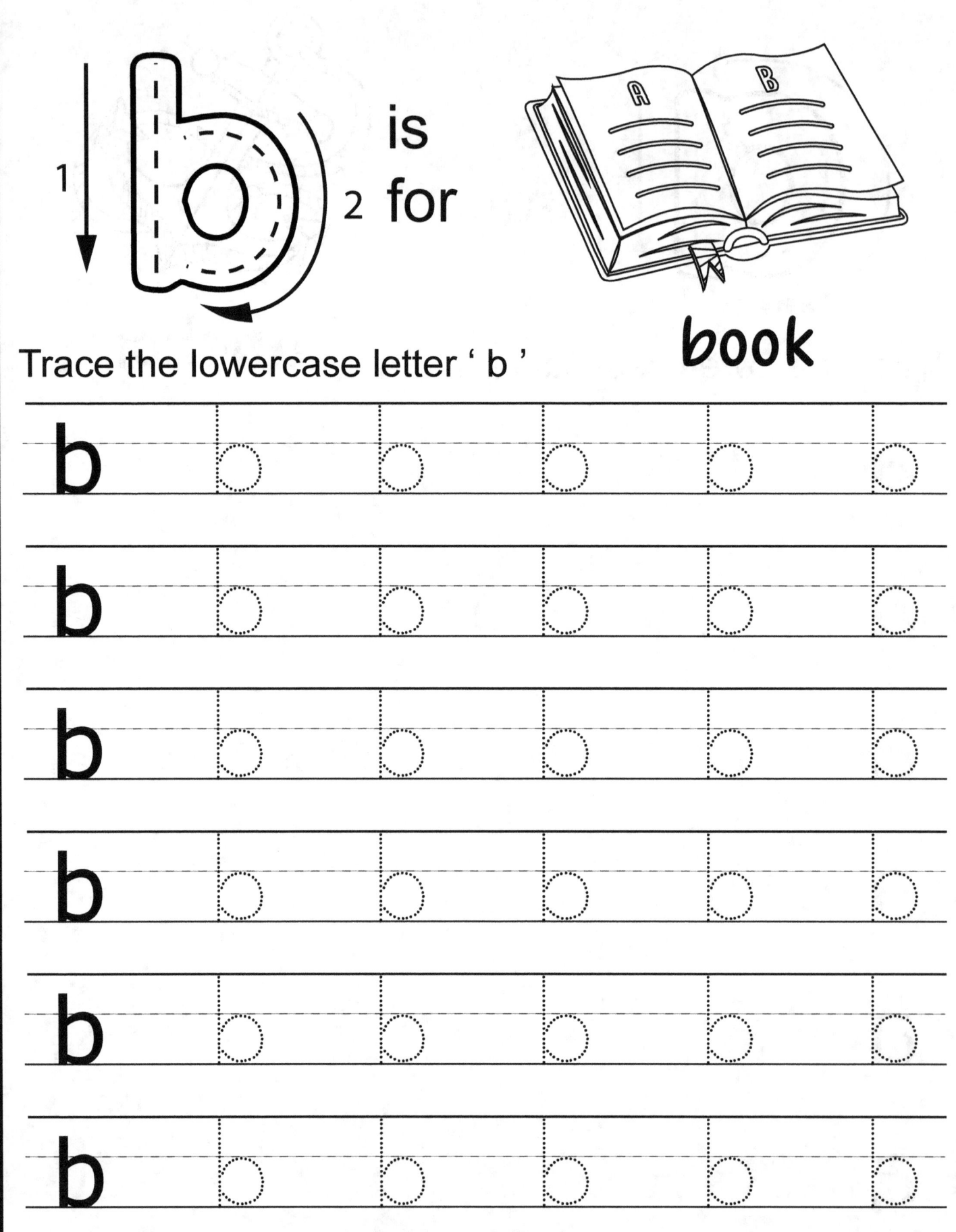

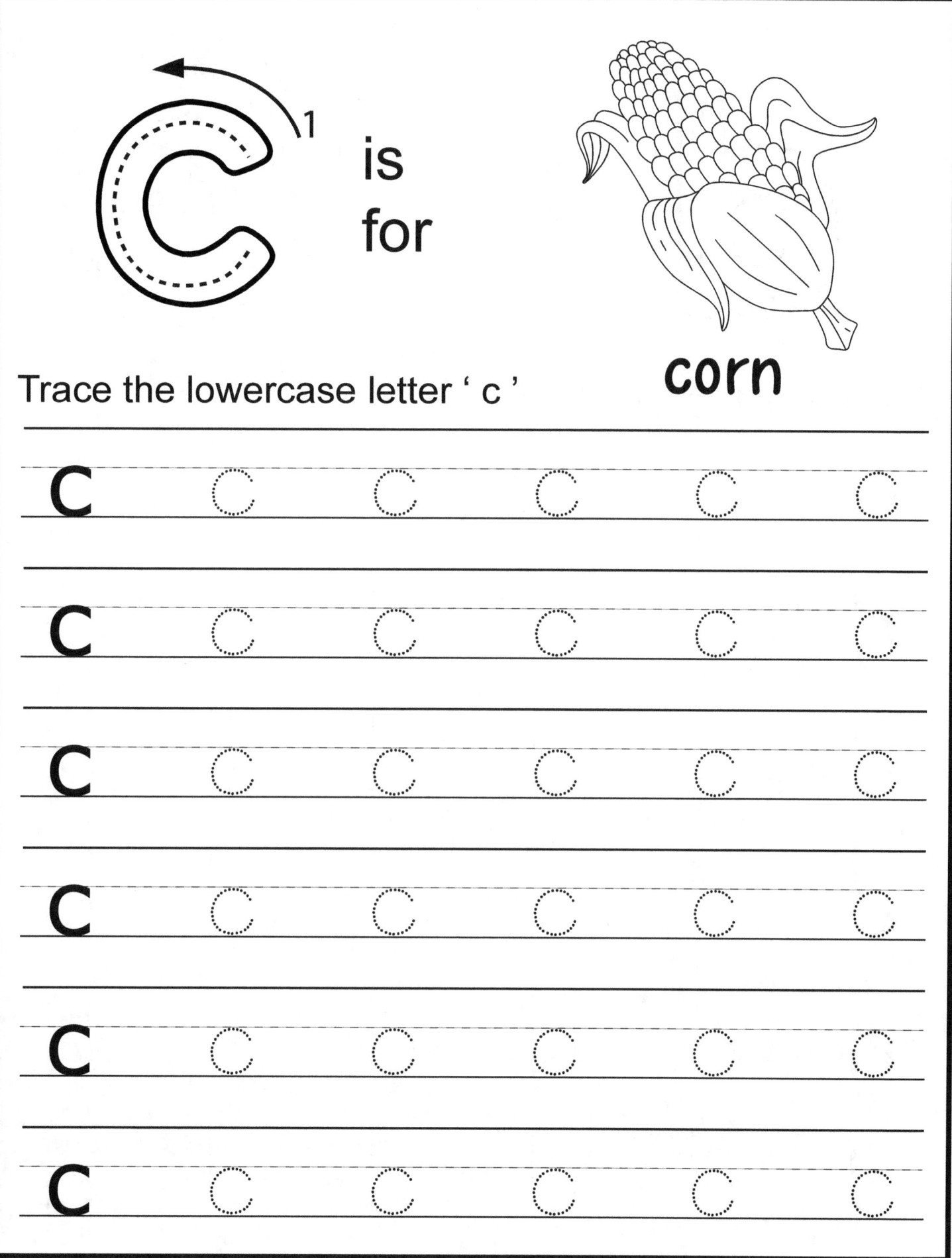

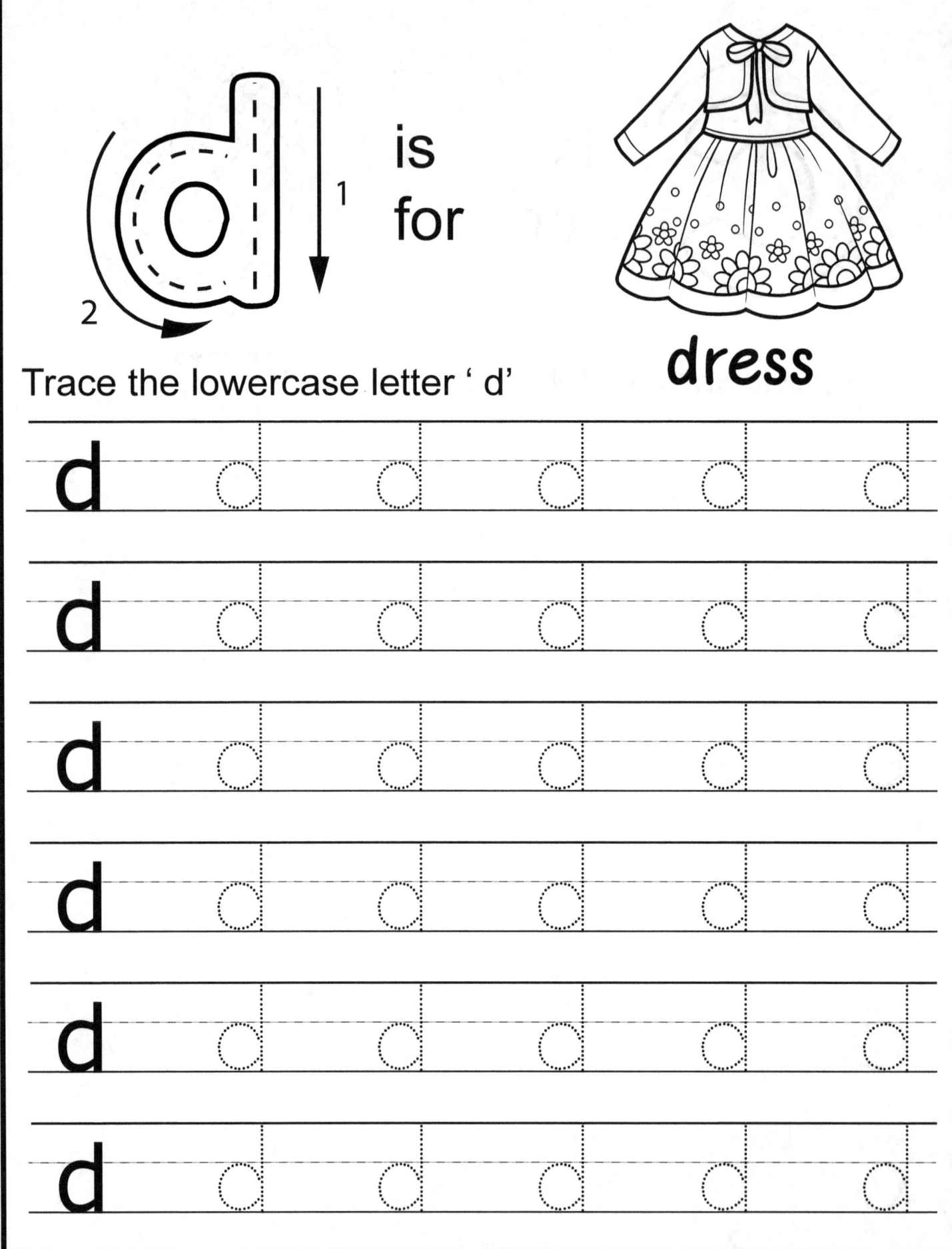

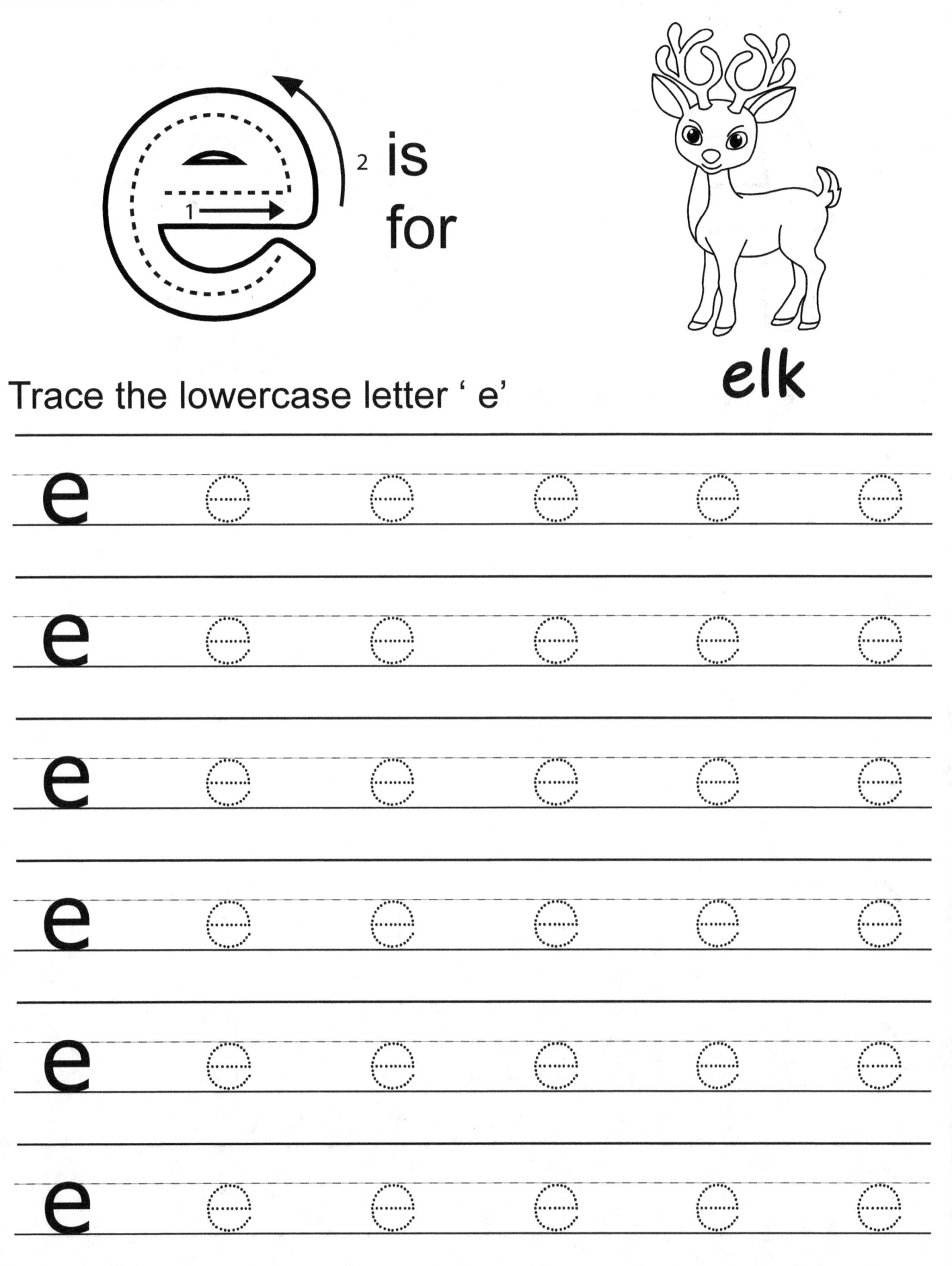

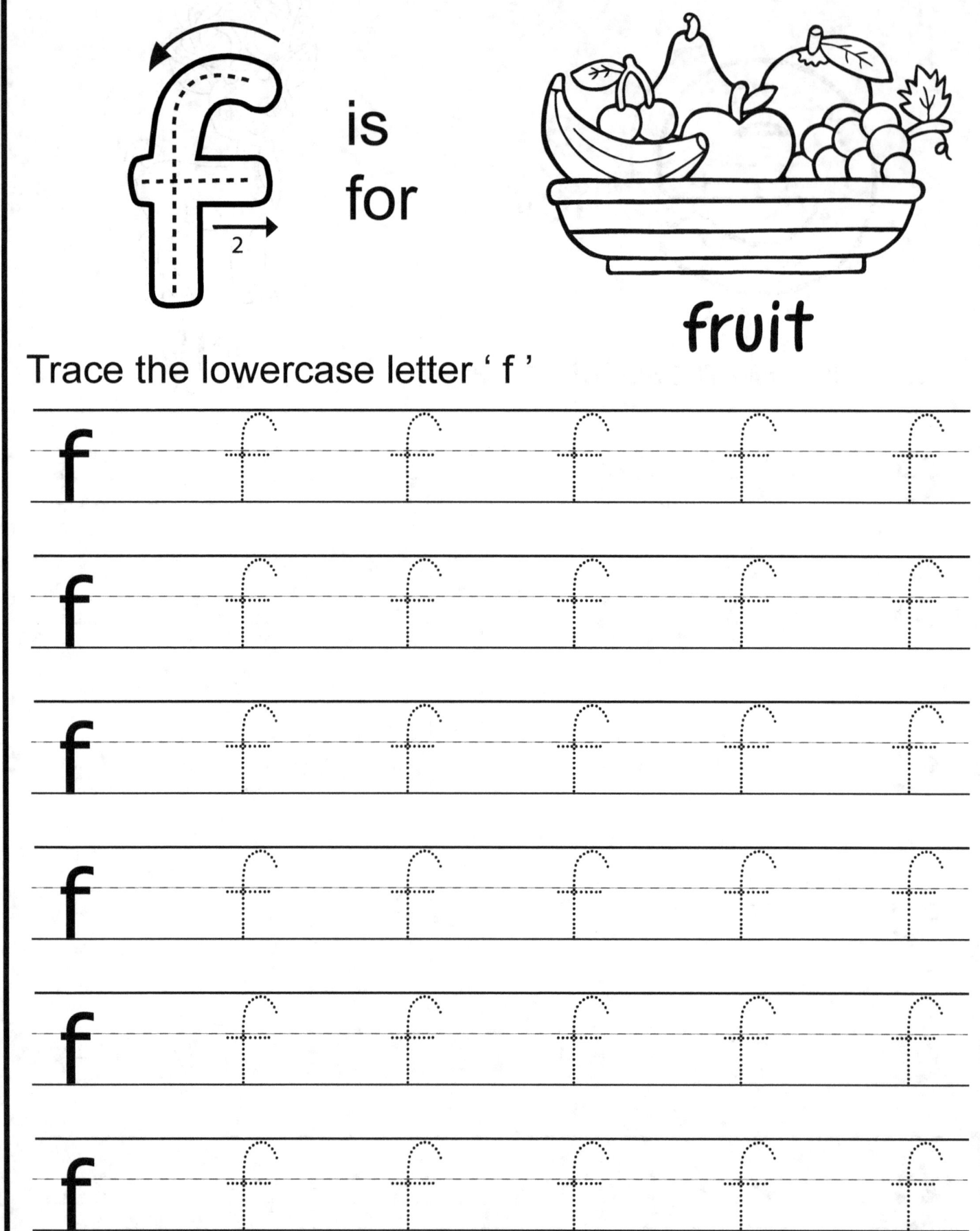

f is for fruit

Trace the lowercase letter ' f '

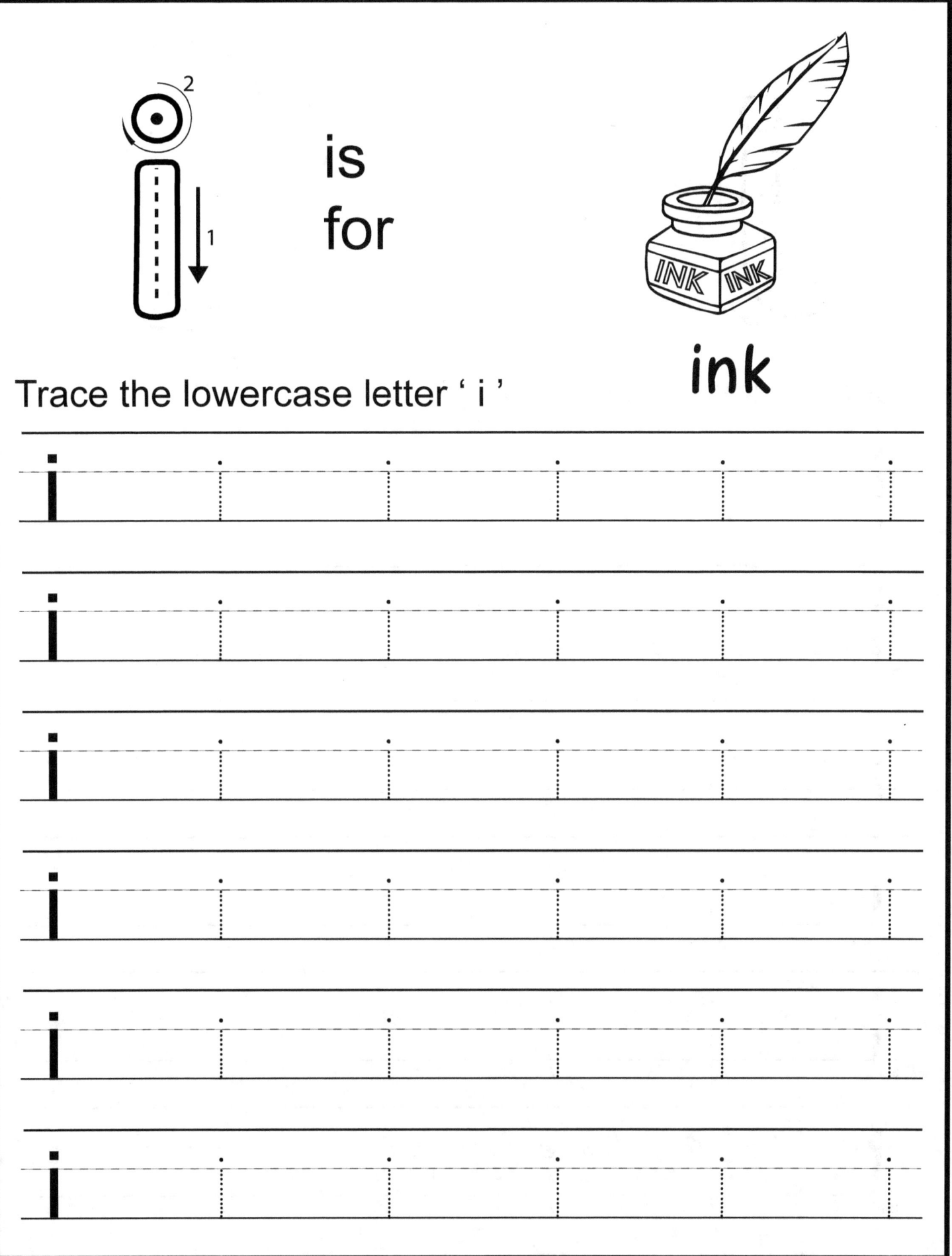

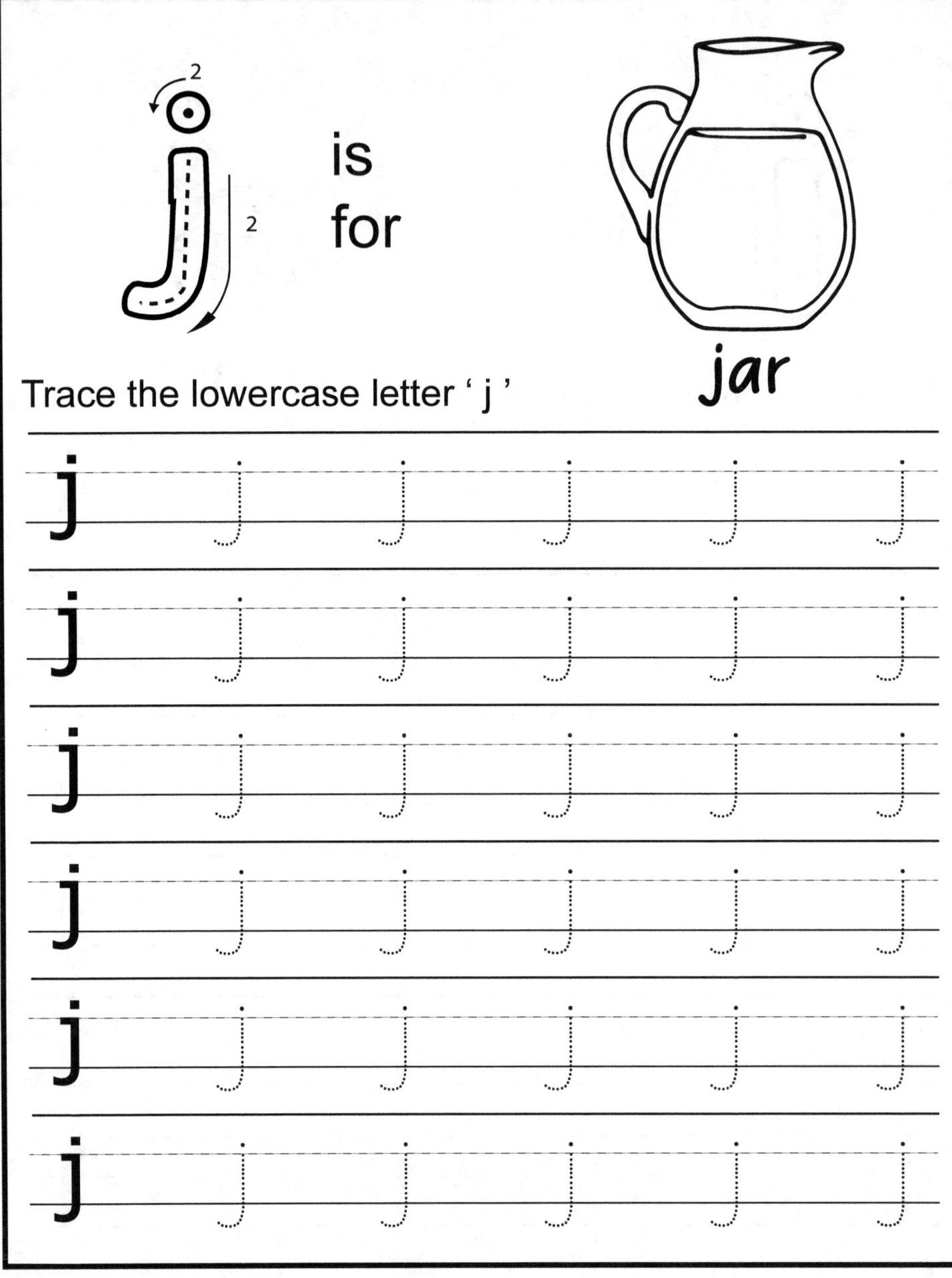

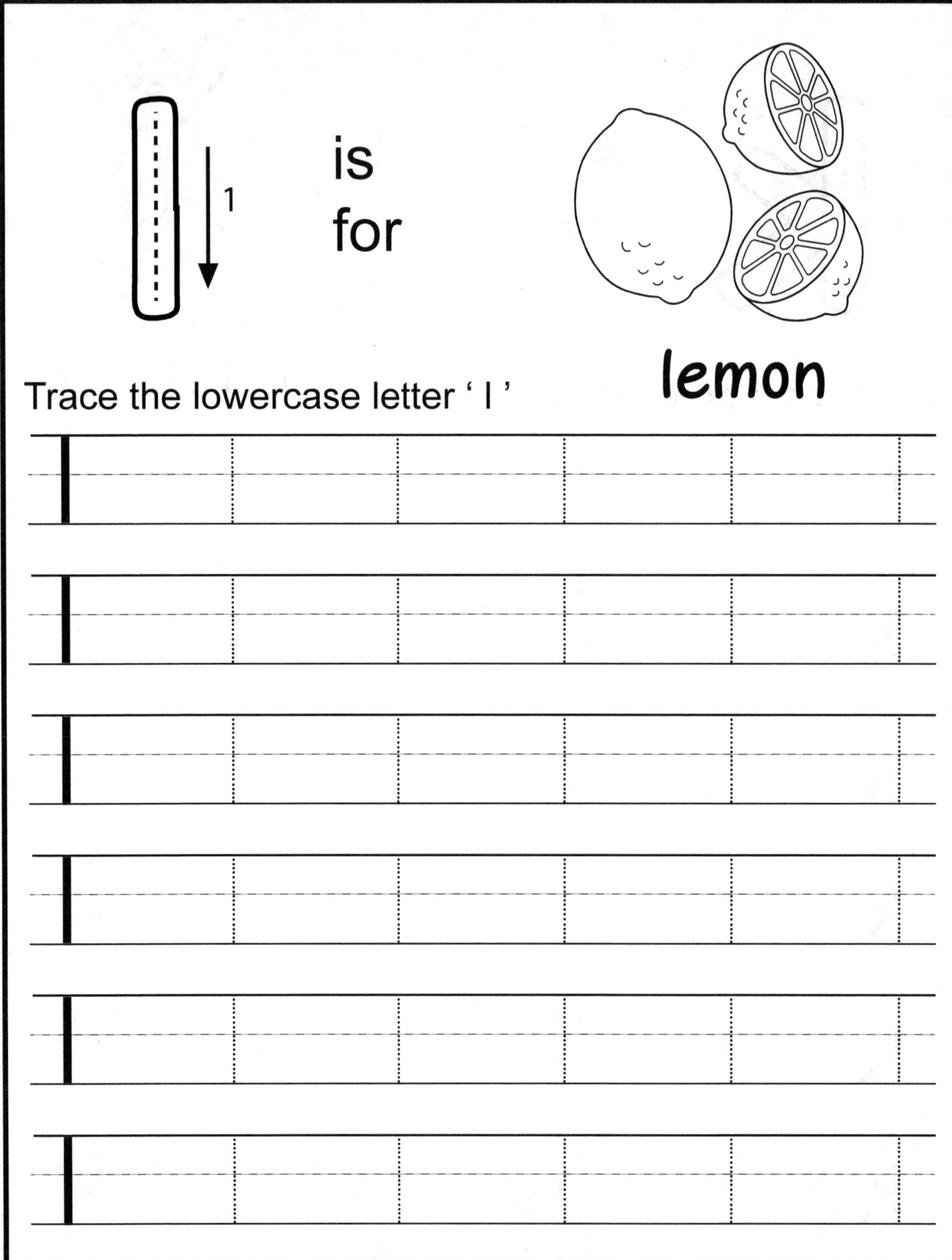

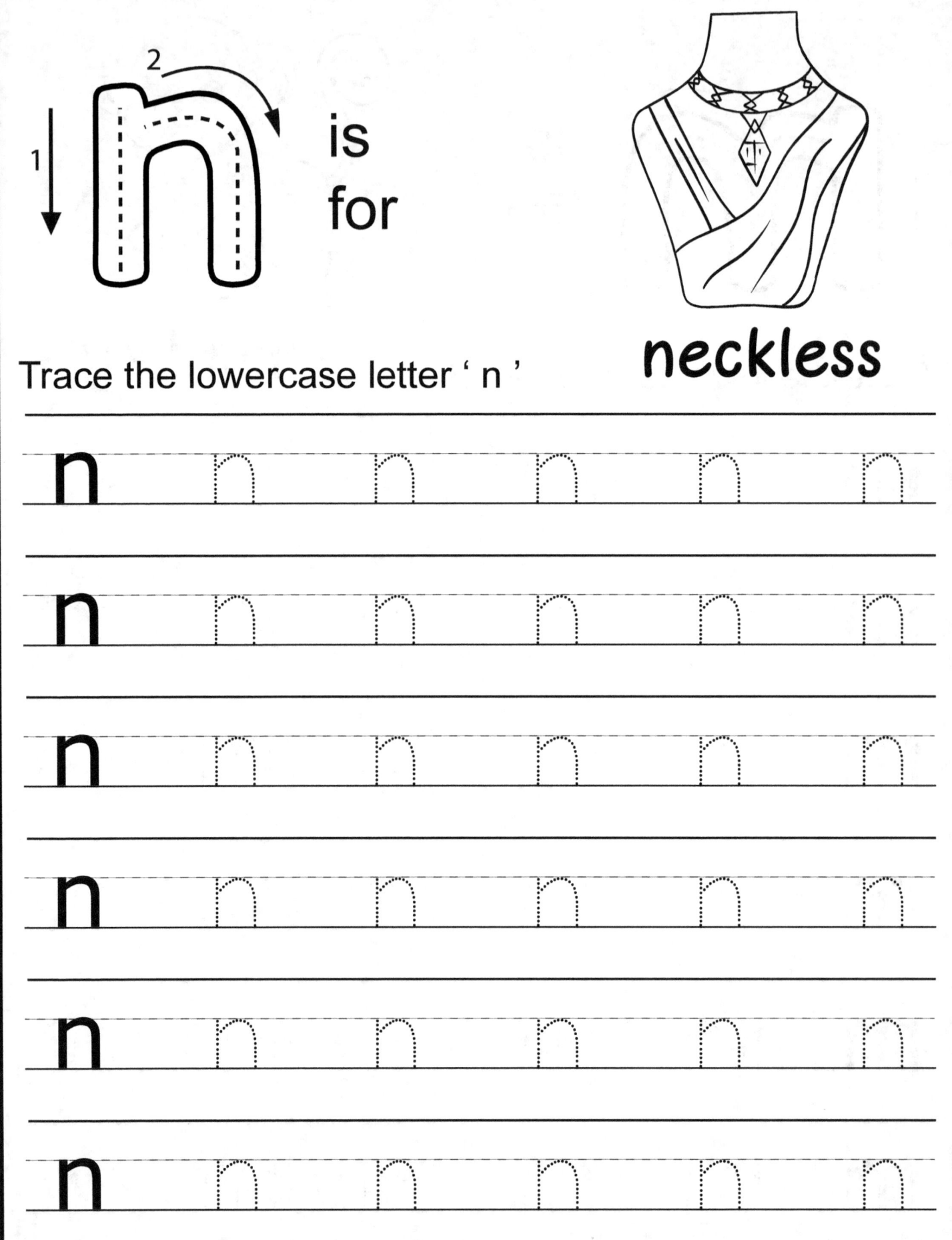

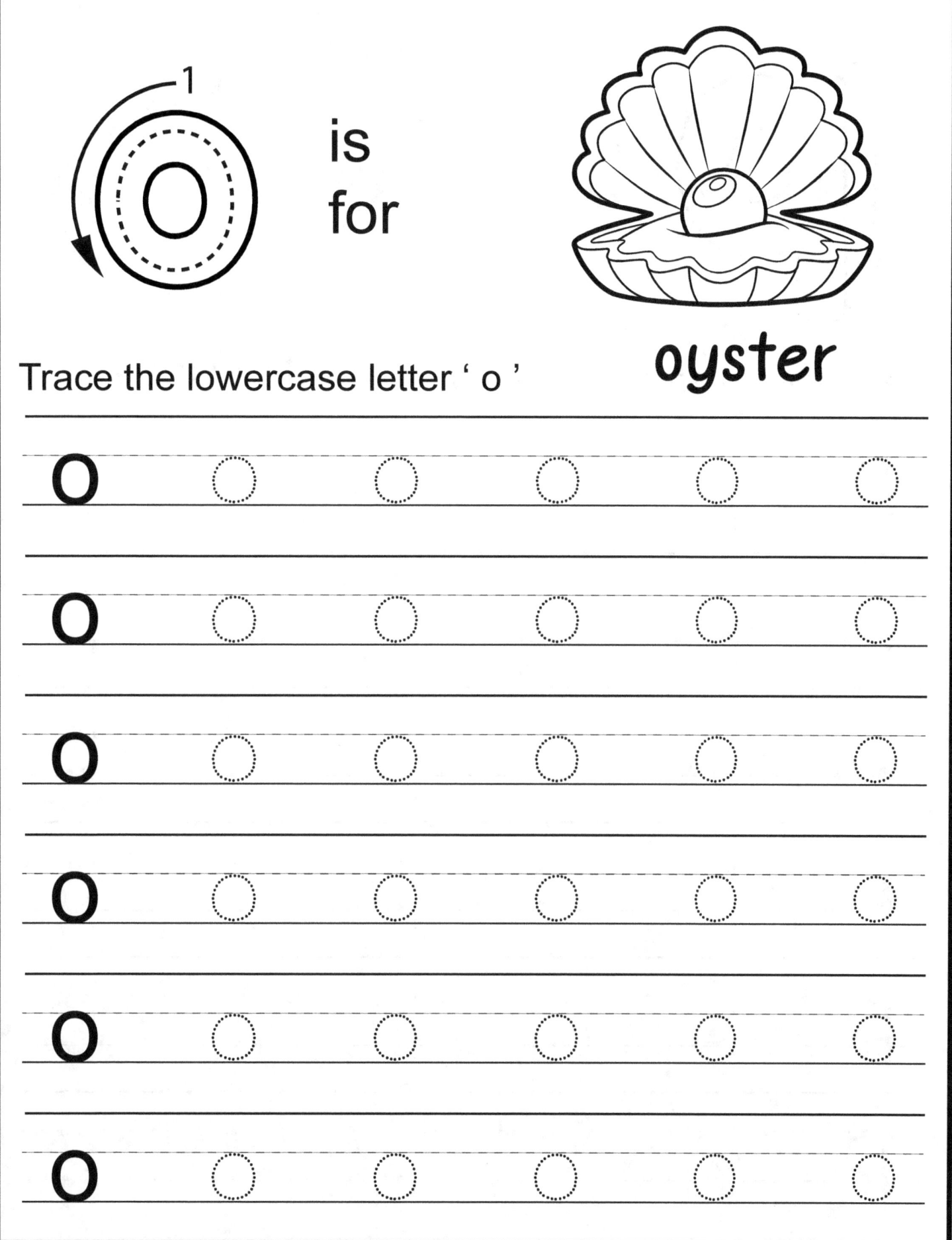

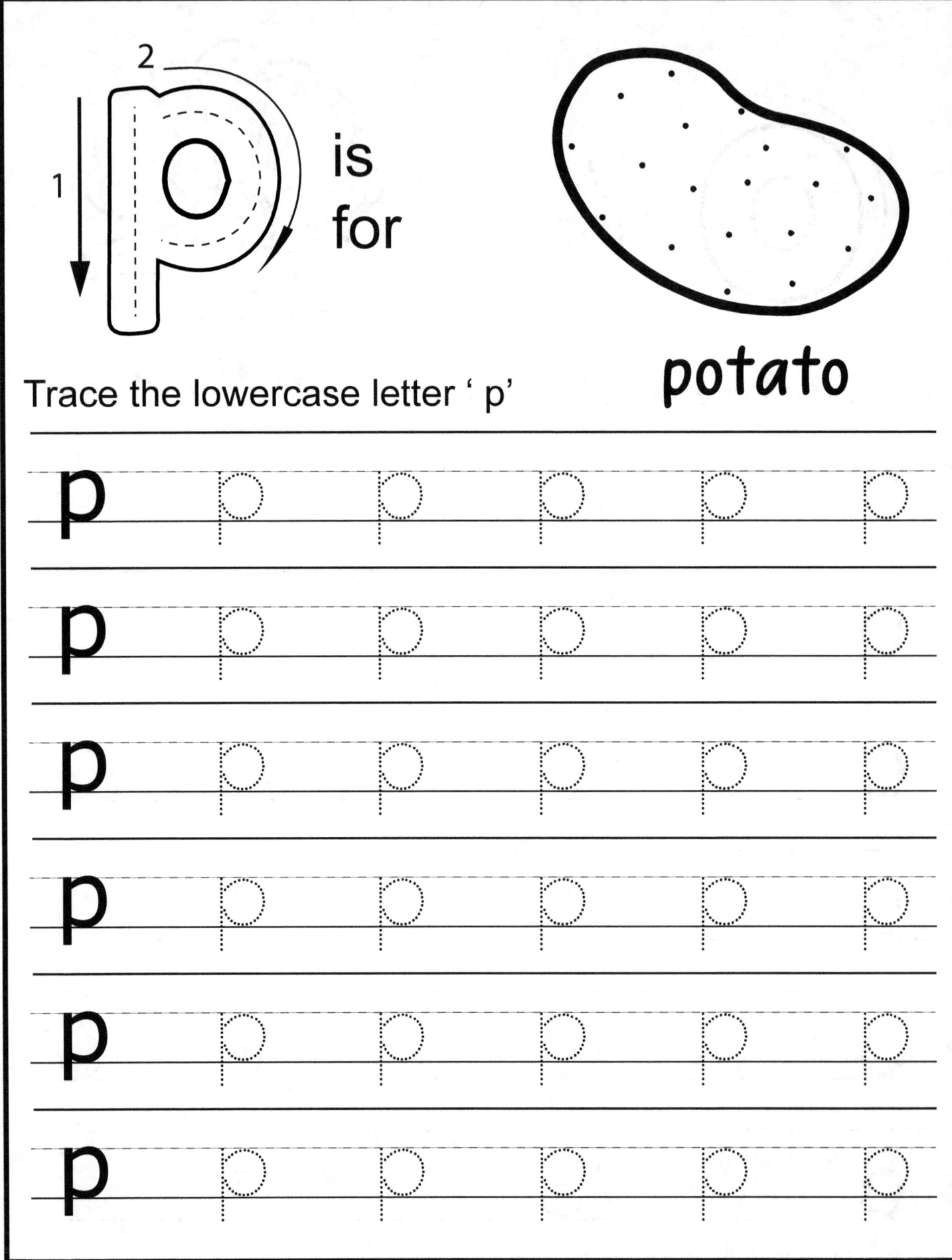

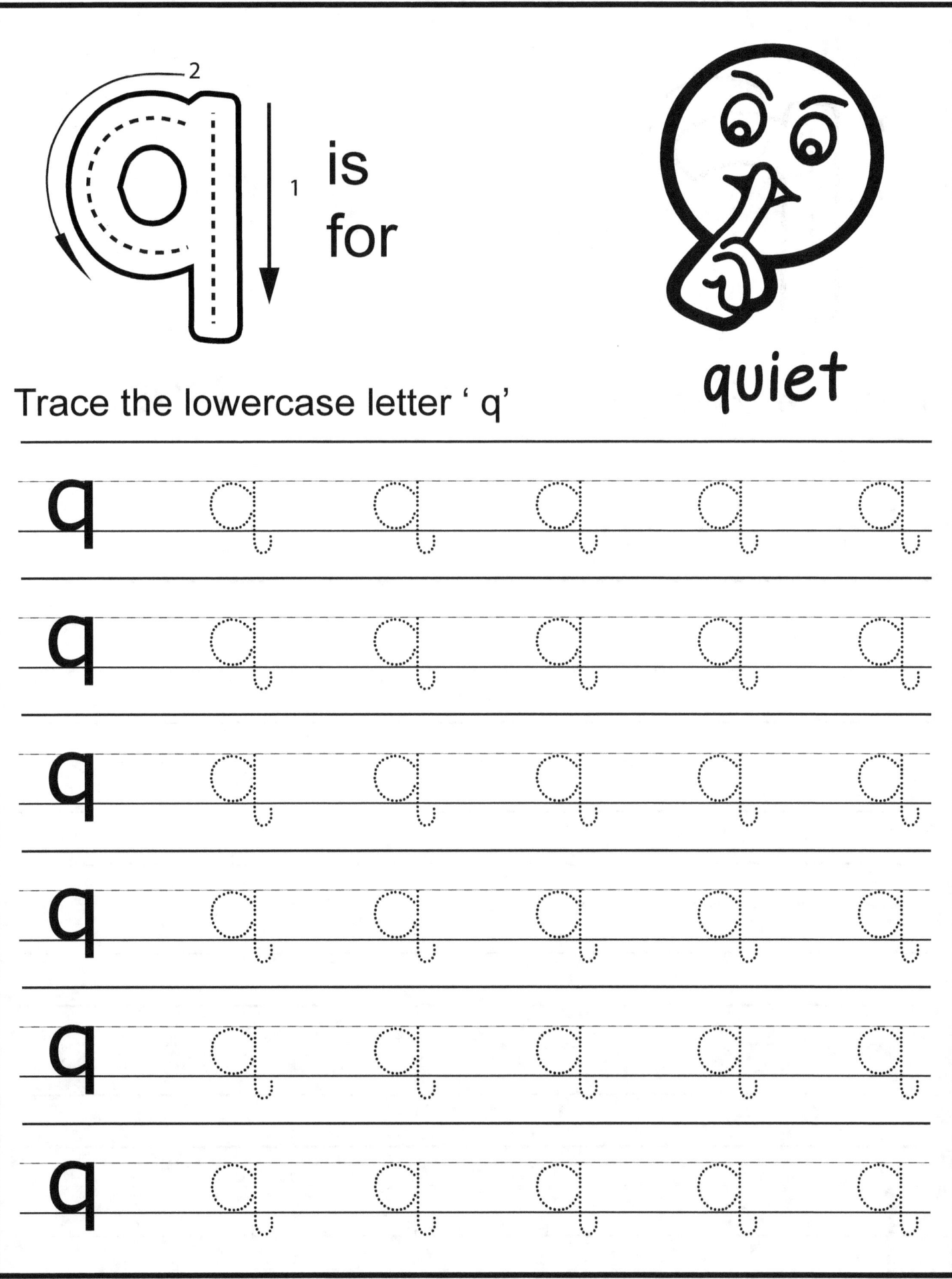

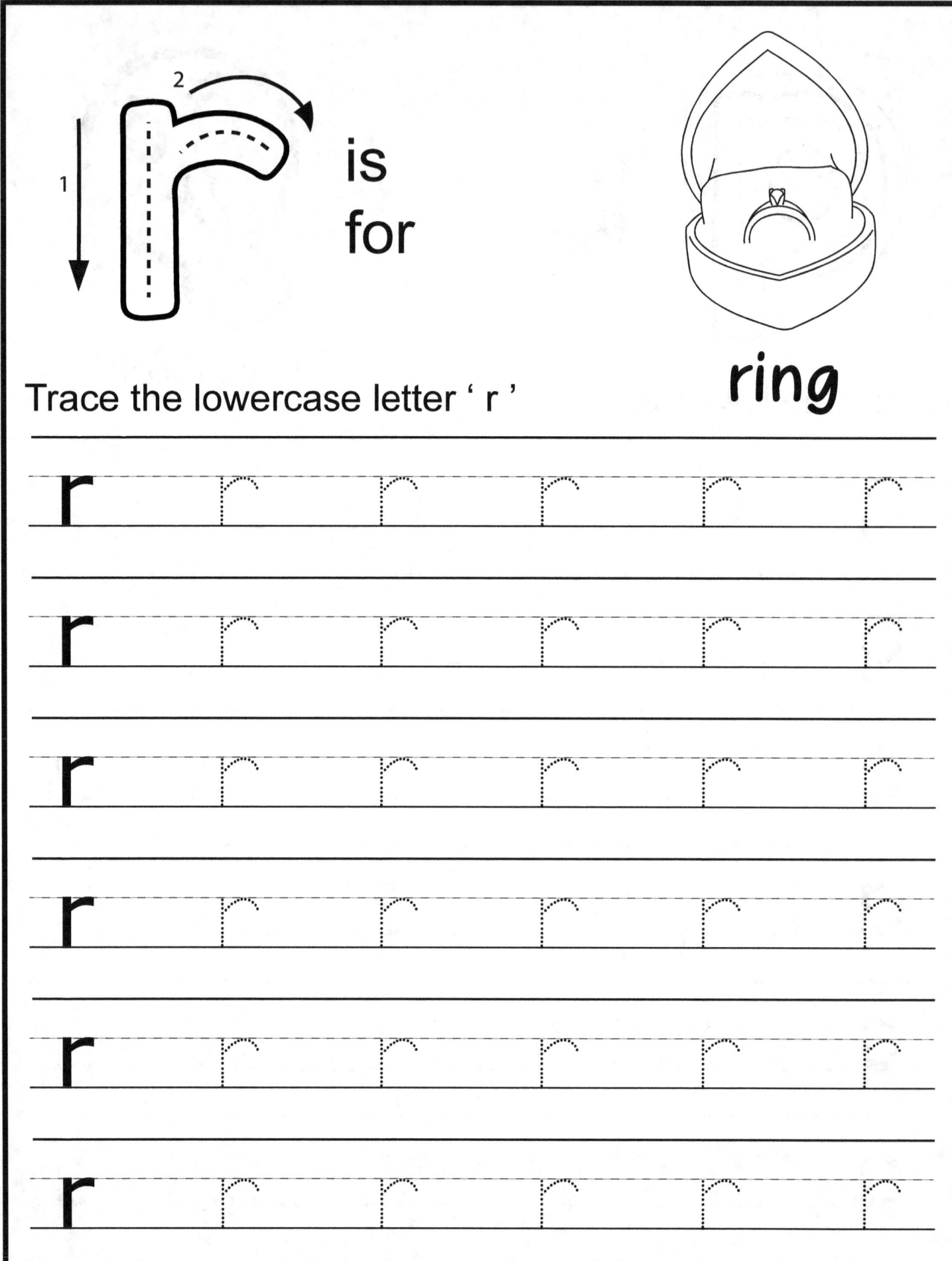

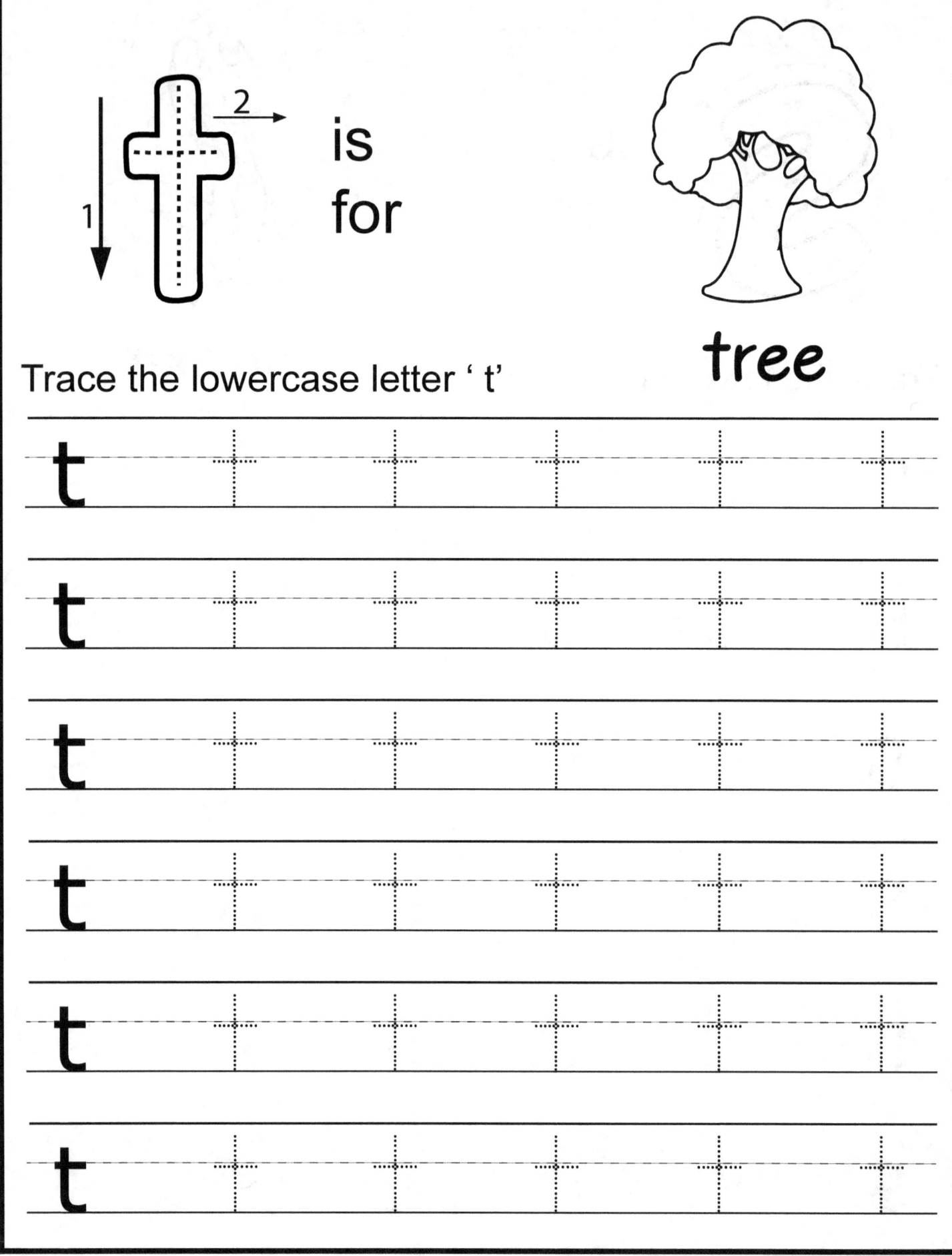

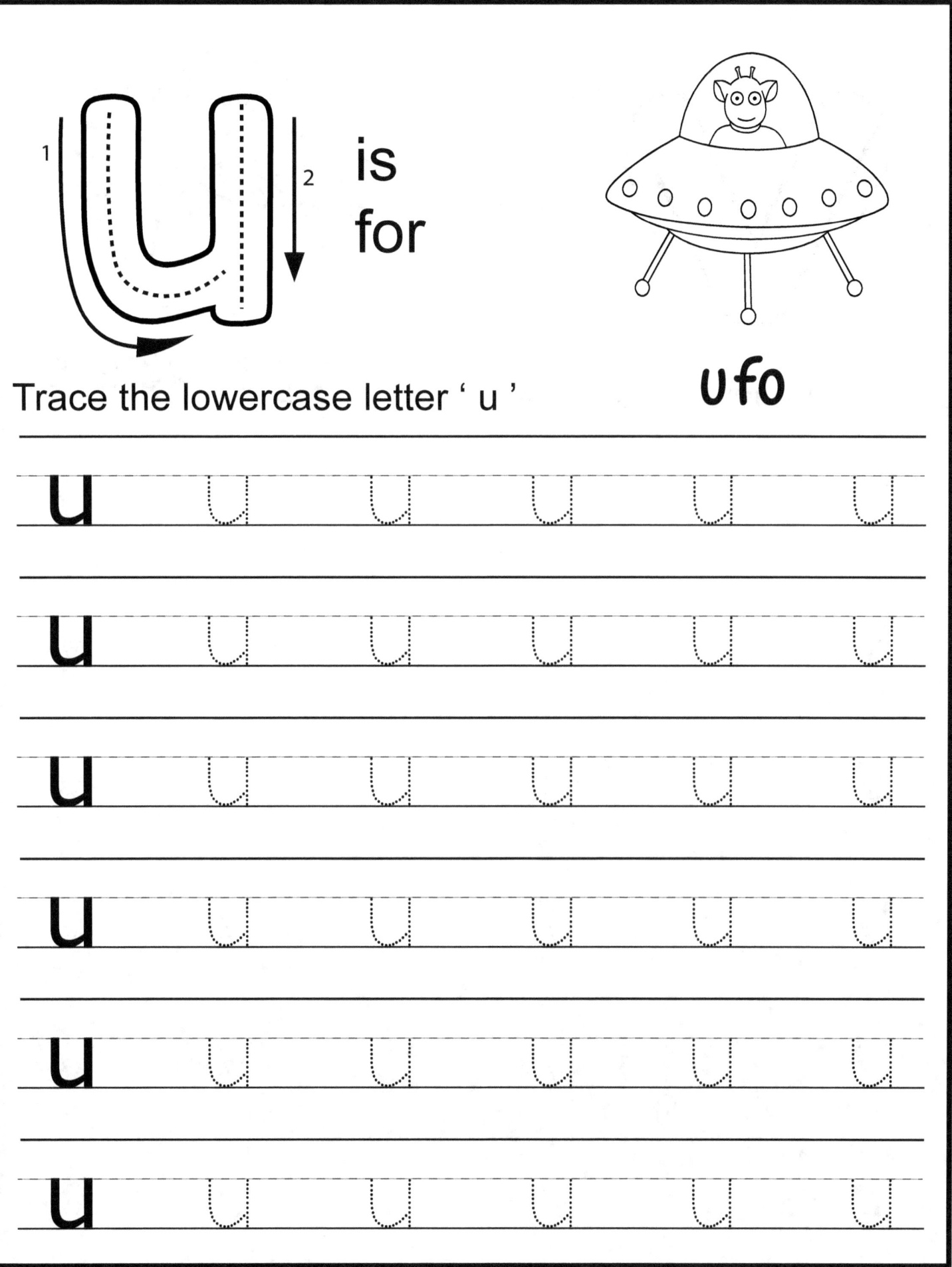

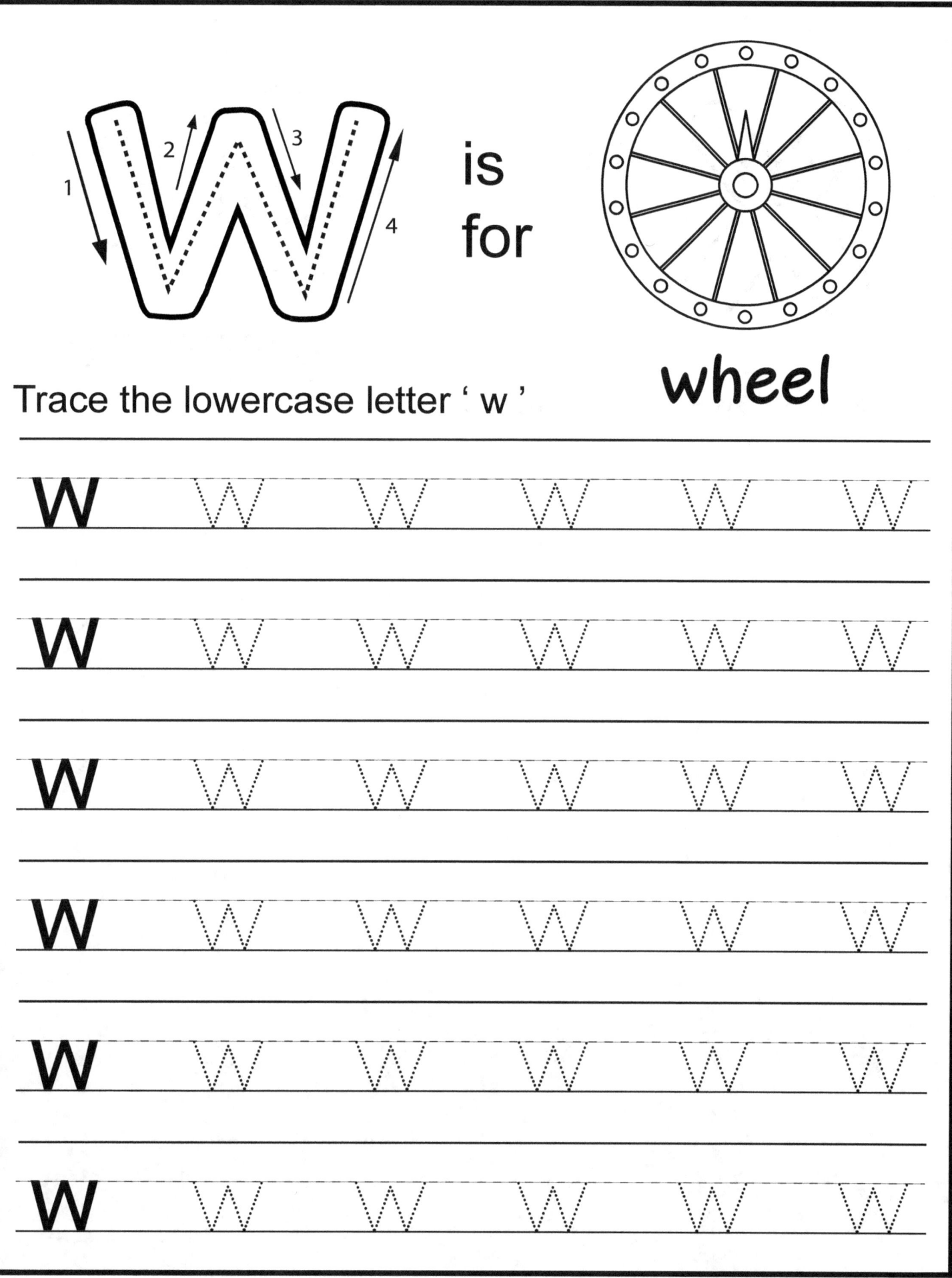

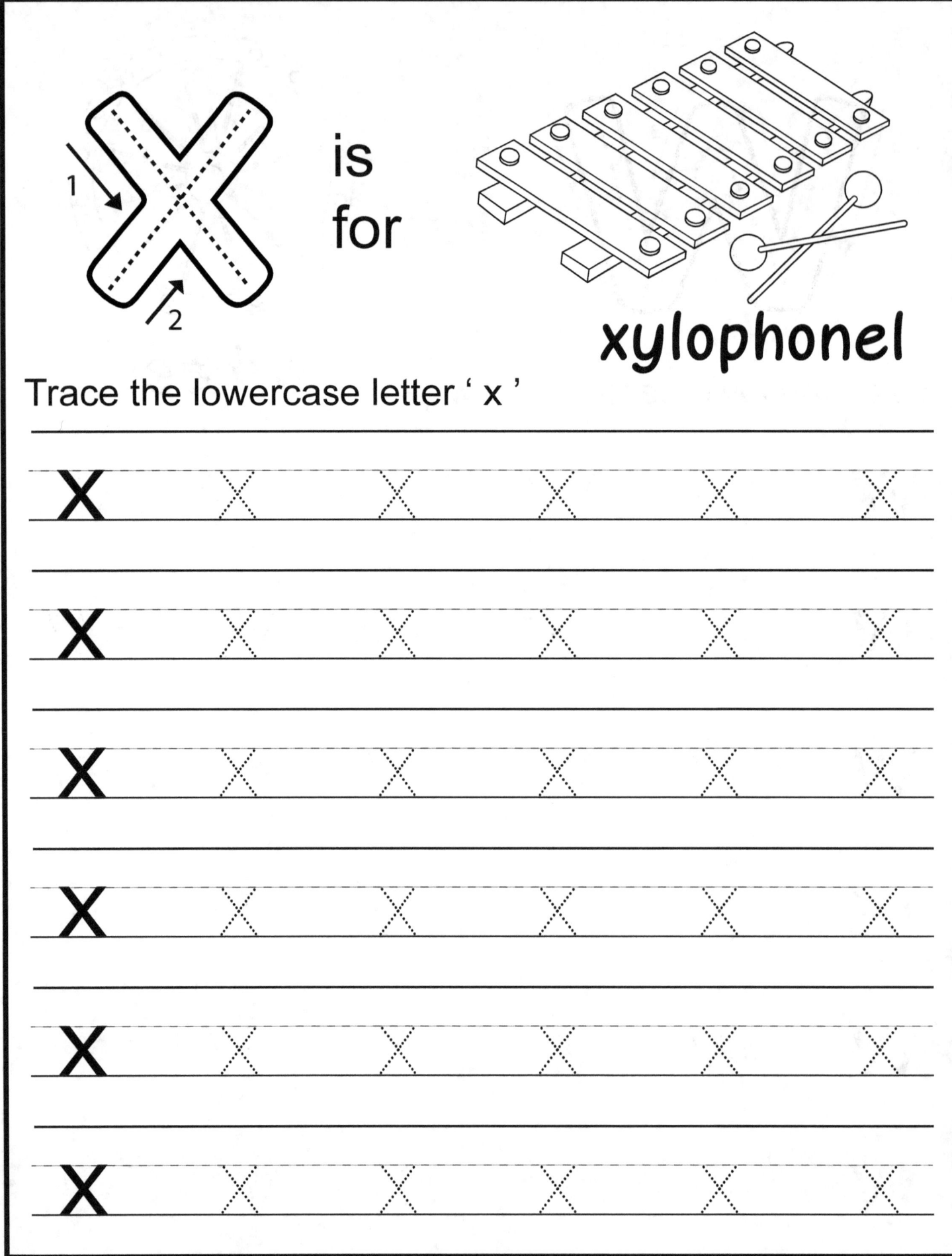

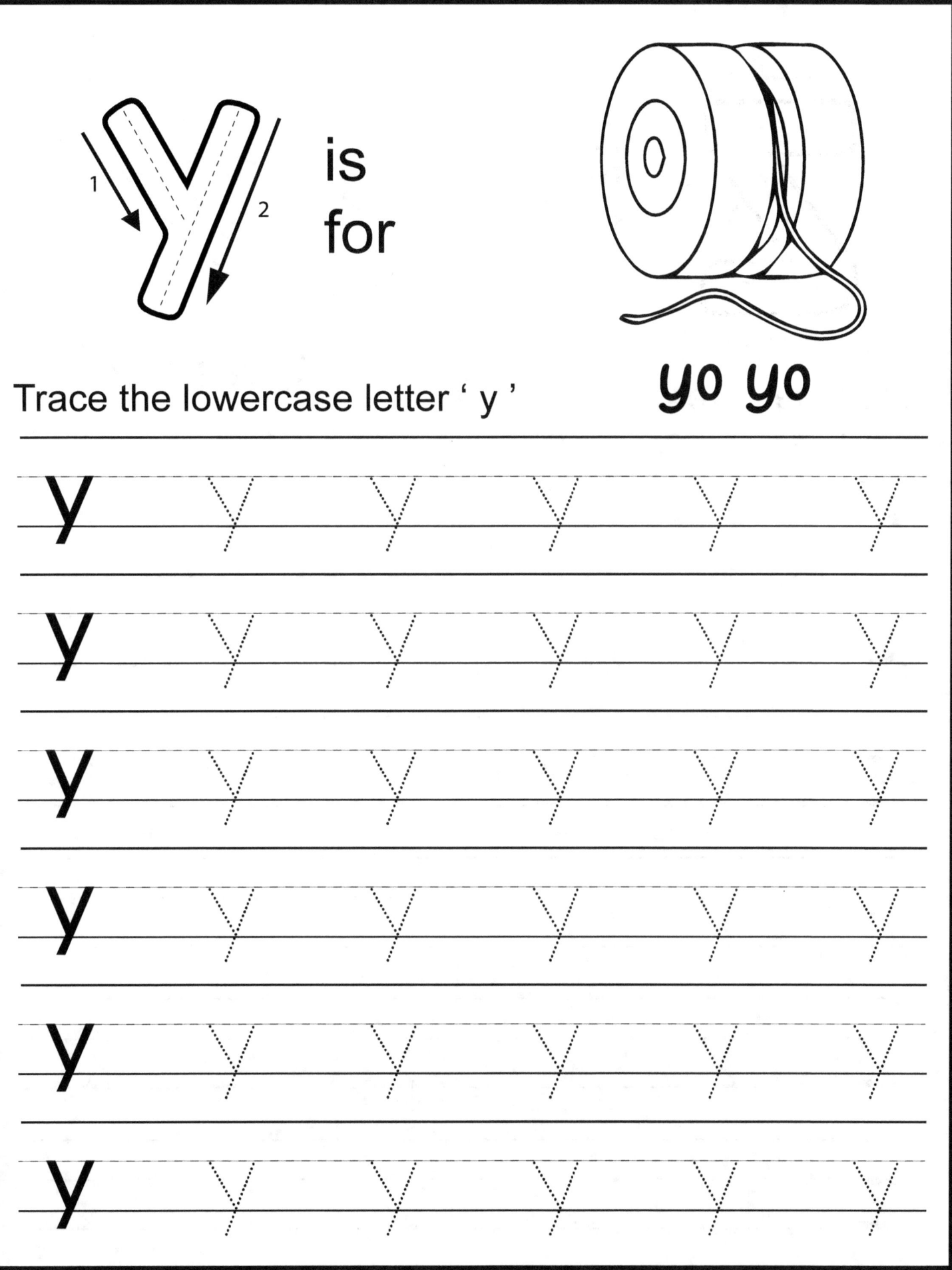

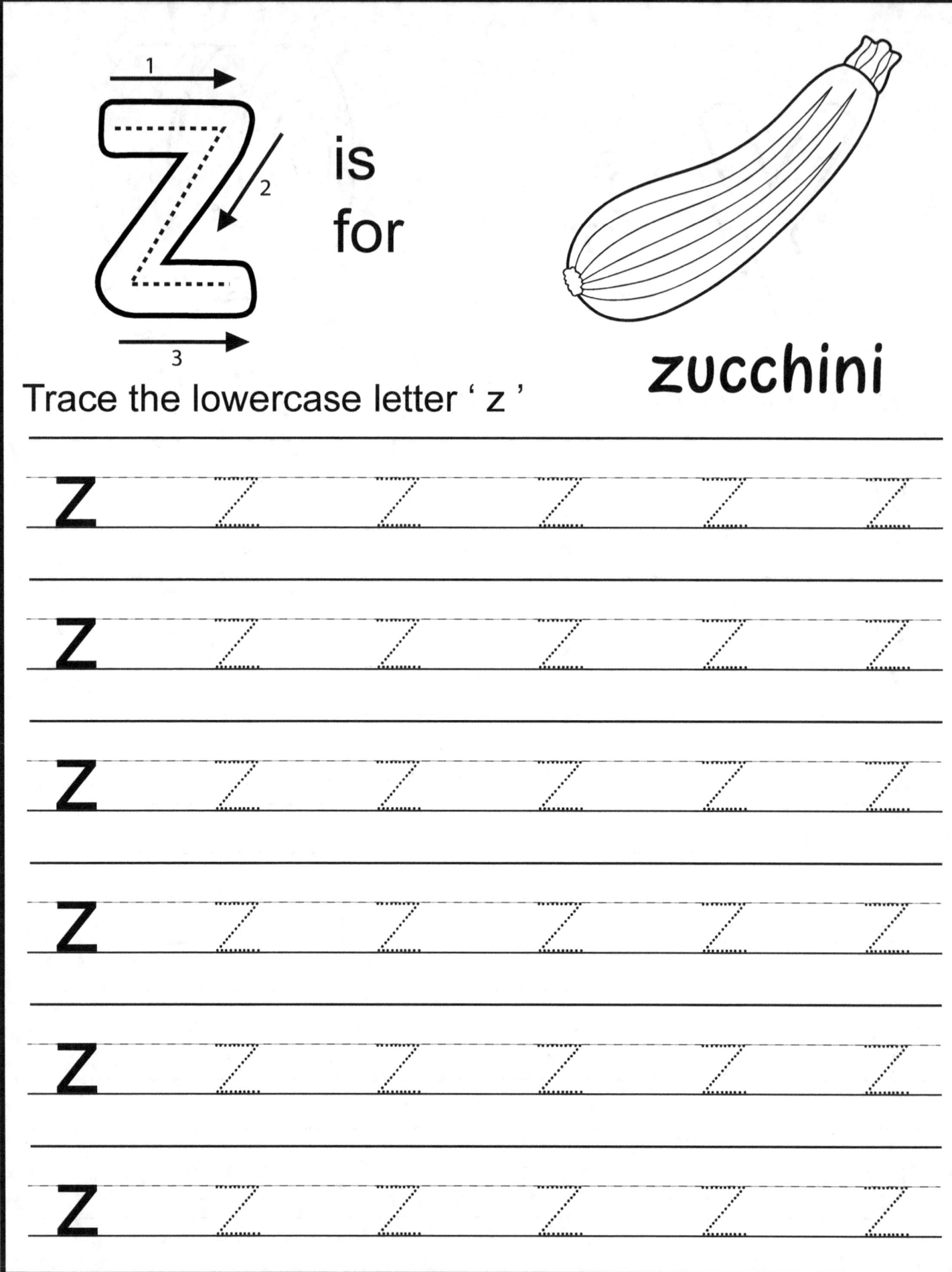

z is for zucchini

Trace the lowercase letter ' z '

z
z
z
z
z
z